CAPTIVE BODIES, FREE SPIRITS

The Story of Southern Slavery

About the Author

Dr. William J. Evitts survived a peripatetic early childhood (six different cities before he was eight years old) until his family settled in Arlington, Virginia, which he considers his hometown. After graduating from public schools, he accepted a scholarship to The Johns Hopkins University, where he received both his B.A. (1964) and his Ph.D. in History (1971). He also holds an M.A. in history from the University of Virginia.

For fifteen years he chaired both the History Department and the American Studies Program at Hollins College, Virginia, where he was also Assistant to the President from 1979 to 1982. His teaching responsibilities included History of the South and Afro-American History. Since 1983 he has been back at Johns Hopkins as Director of Alumni Relations.

Dr. Evitts is married and has two children, Michael and Elizabeth. This book began when he couldn't find anything for them to read to help them understand America's slave past. "Well," said his patient wife, Carole, "write it yourself." So he did.

This is his second book, his first for young people.

Captive Bodies, Free Spirits

THE STORY OF SOUTHERN SLAVERY

William J. Evitts

Julian Messner
New York

This one's for
Mike and Elizabeth

JULIAN MESSNER and colophon are
trademarks of Simon & Schuster, Inc.

10 9 8 7 6 5 4 3 2 1

Photographs courtesy Library of Congress except
pages 64, 105, 111, courtesy National Archives.

Manufactured in the United States of America

Library of Congress Cataloging in Publication Data

Evitts, William J.
  Captive bodies, free spirits.

  Bibliography: p.
  Includes index.
  Summary: Traces the history of slavery in the United
States from the seventeenth century through the Civil
War in 1865 when the institution of slavery was
finally abolished.
    1. Slavery—Southern States—History—Juvenile
literature. [1. Slavery—Southern States—History]
I. Title.
E441.E84 1985   305.8'96'075   85-13922
ISBN 0-671-54094-7

Contents

Introduction

SLAVERY EXISTED IN the United States from the middle of the 1600s until the adoption of the Thirteenth Amendment to the Constitution at the end of the Civil War in 1865. There was no slavery in America at first, but by the time of the American Revolution in 1775, slavery was legal in all thirteen colonies. In the South—Maryland, Virginia, North Carolina, South Carolina, and Georgia—slavery was a powerful part of the economy and the daily lives of the people. How and why slavery grew like this is part of our story.

Slavery slowly disappeared in the North after the American Revolution. Agriculture was always the main use for slavery, but the states north of Maryland eventually moved into manufacturing and trade. Immigrants poured into the northern states. These states grew and changed. But the South kept on in its old ways, sticking to farming and extensively using slaves. By 1860 there were almost four million slaves in the South.

As early as 1820 the North and the South began to argue seriously over slavery. Many in the North wanted slavery to stay where it was and spread no further. Others thought slavery was so evil they wanted to abolish it entirely, even in the states where it had existed for 150 years. As the United States grew, North and South battled for control of each new state or territory that joined the Union. Texas had slavery; should it be let in? What about Kansas and Nebraska? Some Northerners helped slaves run away from the South, or hid them when the Southerners wanted them back. By 1860, North and South were very angry with each other, and although there were many reasons why, slavery was the biggest single cause.

In 1861, civil war broke out between the two sections. It lasted until 1865. When the war began, it was simply about whether or not the South could break away and form a new country. But by the middle of the war, the Northerners were saying that they were also fighting to end slavery. This was the meaning of Abraham Lincoln's Emancipation Proclamation. When the North was victorious in the Civil War, slavery was finally ended in the United States.

Through all of this historical struggle, what about the slaves themselves? How did they live, these four million people? What was it like to be a slave, to be someone's property rather than a person? That is what this book is really about—not just slavery, but slaves. This is their story, told in their own words much of the time, their own deeds.

CHAPTER 1

The Man in the Box

HENRY BROWN HAD a craving for freedom. It burned in him like a fire, consuming his every thought.

Henry Brown was not behind bars in jail. No chains hung from his feet; no handcuffs bound his wrists. But as he walked down the streets of Richmond, Virginia, in the year 1849, Henry Brown was not free. Like almost every other black person he saw on his walk, he was a slave. Another man, a white man, owned Henry Brown, owned him just as you would own a table, or a chair, or a cow.

That was the beginning of what it meant to be a slave. Someone owned you. That was the law. The person owned not only the right to your labor, but *all* of you. If you were a slave, you had to do what your owner said. Your owner could sell you, rent you, give you away, leave you to his or her children in a will, punish you, cheat you—whatever he or she wished. You were property. Even if a slave could walk freely about the city, as Henry Brown could, slavery went with him like an invisible cage. And Henry Brown could stand it no more.

Brown's situation was rather special. Most slaves lived out in the country on farms or large plantations. But Henry Brown was skilled; he was an expert on curing, mixing, and selling tobacco—a tobacconist. His owner let him work in Richmond because Brown could earn more money that way than he could working in the fields. And whatever a slave earned legally belonged to the master, not to the slave. Henry got to keep only a small amount of his pay. But it was not just the money that made Henry hungry for freedom.

Brown's master was not being fair to him. Brown was married, and his wife was the slave of another white man. He could see his wife only with the permission of both masters, and then only after his day's work as a tobacconist was over. Worse, his wife's owner was thinking of selling her to a place far away, a cotton plantation in the deep South. Marriage meant nothing in slave law. Brown was powerless. He had pleaded with his own master to help him save his wife, but the man refused.

Brown's one hope was to buy his wife from the other master. He had saved carefully from his tiny allowance, but years of work had left him only $166. That was far too little.

This final shame, this terrible injustice, was what finally pushed Henry Brown to decide. He would sacrifice anything not to be a slave anymore. He would be free or die trying.

His trip down the street took him to a store where he knew the shopkeeper, a white man who had become his friend. As he went in, he looked around, and he saw with relief that the two of them were alone. Gathering up his courage, Brown did a dangerous thing. He told the white man that he was going to try to escape. He asked for help.

THE MAN IN THE BOX

If the shopkeeper had wished, he could have had the slave arrested, or sent back to his owner and punished. Brown was risking jail, or a whipping, or being sold far away, or all of those things. He was that desperate. So he asked for help, held his breath, and waited.

"Are you not afraid to speak to me this way?" the white man asked cautiously.

"No," said Henry, "I imagine you believe that every man has a right to liberty."

"Yes," the shopkeeper agreed, "you are quite right."

The man agreed to help. But it would cost Henry half of all that he had painfully saved to get the man's assistance.

Brown's next step was to see another friendly white man, a Dr. Smith, for more help and advice. Dr. Smith listened to several of Henry's escape plans, but none seemed satisfactory. Richmond was nearly 200 miles from the nearest state, Pennsylvania, where slavery was not legal and where Brown might be safe. Even there he could be captured and returned, but Pennsylvania was at least "free" territory and outside the South. People there did not expect every black man on the street to be a slave. But how was he to get there? Blacks who traveled were always under suspicion in the South. He would be questioned. Police would ask to see his freedom papers, and of course he had none. Danger and doubt clouded his mind. As he left Dr. Smith, he still had no workable plan. All he had was a fierce determination.

It came to him as he worked. He stopped, and in his own words, this is what he said: "I felt my soul called out to Heaven to breathe a prayer to Almighty God . . . that

He . . . would lend me His aid." And, "in a flash," the idea was formed. He would have himself crated up and sent to Philadelphia. He would actually mail himself to freedom. He was being treated like a piece of goods; very well, then, he would be shipped just like merchandise.

A Richmond carpenter made the box, probably without knowing its purpose. A merchant in Philadelphia was let in on the plan and was ready to receive the "goods."

Now Brown needed time—time to get on his way and be long gone before he was missed. He decided to fake an illness that would keep him from work. He had an injured finger, but it was not serious enough. Dr. Smith gave him some acid to damage the finger even more, and when Brown accidentally put on too much, he produced a painful wound. The finger was, in his own words, "eaten in to the bone." The pain was awful, but Brown knew the pain of slavery was worse. His ruined hand bought him the time he needed.

At four o'clock in the morning of March 29, 1849, Dr. Smith and the shopkeeper secretly sealed Henry Brown into a wooden crate measuring three feet long, two feet wide, and two feet deep. He was crouched, in a sort of sitting position. He had three small air holes, a tool for drilling more air holes just in case, and a flask of water. His friends took him to the express office. Brown's incredible escape had begun.

The journey of Henry Brown became a nightmare. Despite instructions on the box to keep "This end up," the first baggage handlers turned the crate upside down, leaving Brown on his head. At the Richmond depot he was thrown roughly from the wagon and landed lying on his right side. No one jostling the heavy crate had any idea of the astonishing contents, that a live man was curled up inside. And no matter what, Henry Brown had to clench his teeth and make no sound at all.

He rode on his side to the Potomac River landing, where the box was moved to a steamboat for the journey to Washington, DC. Someone stacked the box upside down again. Very soon the head-down position became almost unbearable. Blood rushed to Brown's head. His veins pounded with pressure. He could feel his eyes bulging out of their sockets. He could not move his arms. A cold sweat came over him. He endured half an hour, then an hour, then more. The pain was horrible. He began to think he would die. He even wished he would. In his agony, he began to pray. Two hours had passed when his throbbing ears faintly heard a baggage man complain that he had been standing the whole way and was tired, he needed a place to sit. The other handler said, "Sit on the box." And with that, the first man turned Brown's crate on its side, for a better seat. Henry Brown's prayer was answered, and for the moment his pain was over.

"What do you suppose is in this box?" one man asked.

Henry Brown held his breath.

"I guess it's the mail," replied the other man.

Inside his cramped wooden prison, Brown managed a smile. Mail, indeed, but not at all what the men would have guessed.

Trouble began again in Washington. The city was the capital of the United States, but it still had slavery. Henry Brown's trip was barely half over.

A nineteenth-century lithograph showing Henry "Box" Brown being uncrated in Philadelphia.

He was upright in a wagon when he reached the train station. Voices called back and forth as men moved the freight. A man wanted help with Brown's box, but no one would come. Ignoring the "handle with care" instructions, the angry worker finally tumbled the box off the back of the wagon. It dropped several feet and Brown landed head first. He heard a cracking noise in his neck and lost consciousness.

As he slowly fought his way back to his senses, the first words Brown heard filled him with fear. The train was full. They would leave the crate overnight on the platform. He knew he could not survive that. At the last moment a worker insisted that a package marked "express" could not wait. Room was found, and he was put on the train, again in the unbearable head-down position. At the last minute before departure, he was shifted to his side to make room for even more luggage.

He endured the pain in his head and his acid-eaten finger during the long train ride to Philadelphia. Finally, he heard voices in the baggage car saying the train was in Philadelphia. He was on free soil, and his heart leapt for joy.

One more unloading, one more wagon ride, and a day and a half after Dr. Smith had driven the nails closing him in the box, Henry Brown was finally at the home of the Philadelphia man who had agreed to help. Still uncertain, Brown kept silent until he heard a rap on the box, and a nervous voice asked, "Is all right within?"

It took a second for Brown to find the power to speak. Finally he rasped out, "All right!"

The small crowd gathered around the crate shouted for joy. In a few moments the box was unsealed. Henry Brown rose, as he later said, "resurrected from the grave of slavery." And as soon as he did, he fainted, overcome by hunger, pain, exhaustion, and the relief from the strain.

As soon as he came to, he led his new friends in a prayer of thanks. Henry Brown's incredible travels were over. He was free.

But millions of black people were still in slavery in the South.

CHAPTER 2

The Birth of
Slavery in America

AT THE TIME of Henry Brown's astonishing journey, the United States had been free from England for seventy-three years. The Declaration of Independence was written in 1776. It said, "All men are created equal," and that all had a basic right to "liberty." How could Brown or anyone else be a slave? How could the country that gave the world this Declaration have allowed one set of persons to own another set of persons?

The puzzle grows because the author of the Declaration, Thomas Jefferson, owned hundreds of slaves himself. And it grows even bigger when you know that as the English first began settling what became the United States, there was no such thing as slavery in English law or tradition.

How could slavery happen here?

First, slavery is a very old idea. The earliest records of human history tell of slaves. They are even mentioned in the Bible. The commonest way for someone to become a slave was to be captured in war. Another way was to be poor and landless and have no other way to live. And, of course, there were always people who would be willing to make other people work for them.

So the first reason for slavery was *economic*. The rich, the powerful, and the victorious took those less fortunate and put them to work as slaves.

Slavery is also easier for the masters if they think that the slaves are inferior people, not as good as the masters are. After all, the masters' reasoning goes, if a group of people are ignorant, or backward, or "savages," or not able to make anything of themselves, isn't it better to put them to work to help people who are superior? That way, the "better" people can take care of the "inferior" people and make something good of them.

The second reason for slavery, then, was *prejudice*— the belief that certain people are not as good as you are.

When the English landed at Jamestown, Virginia, in 1607, they had no real idea what they were starting. They hoped to find local natives with plenty of gold and jewels that the English could trade for, or cheat them out of. But the Indians of North America were not like the Indians the Spanish had plundered in Central and South America. There was no gold.

There was lots of land, however, and Jamestown turned into a farming community. They grew not just food, but tobacco. The smoking craze was sweeping Europe, and tobacco was precious in those days because it was scarce. So even though the English King, James I, angrily called tobacco "the stinking weed," the Jamestowners began to grow it as fast as they could. They also began to grow rich because of it.

Before long, the new Virginia colony had a problem.

CAPTIVE BODIES, FREE SPIRITS

There was lots of land, more than they could possibly use at once. There was big money to be made growing tobacco. But all the Englishmen coming into Virginia wanted to be landowners, not workers in the field. Even if they all worked hard in the fields, there was still too much land and not enough workers. They could all get rich—if only they could get enough workers. But where could these workers come from? They thought of using Indians, but the Native Americans would not give up their free life to work in the white man's fields, and the Indians were too dangerous to try to capture.

The first black servants from Africa came to Virginia in the year 1619. A Dutch ship brought nineteen of them and exchanged them for supplies. They were not called slaves; they were called "servants." Slavery was not known in Virginia yet, but being a servant was. Many landowners and powerful people first came to the New World as servants and then worked their way up. These first black Africans were not considered any different in the beginning.

But it wasn't long before the farmers could see the benefit of having servants who could not leave, could not ask for pay, and had to work for you all their lives. When a servant stays a servant for life, without pay, and has no right to leave or say what hours he works, or how hard, or anything about his life, he has become a slave. That is what happened. After a while black servants were treated differently from white servants. First, the courts in the English colonies began to make different rulings for blacks. Black servants received harder punishments. Then the legislatures made different laws for blacks. In

THE BIRTH OF SLAVERY IN AMERICA

Virginia, for example, when they passed a law protecting servants from having to serve their masters for too long, this law applied only to whites. The laws began to mention "heathen" servants, meaning non-Christian, non-white servants. One state made masters pay a property tax on "heathen female" servants. The next step was to say that African servants could not be set free legally, but had to be servants all of their lives. Then the whites passed a law saying that if a mother was a servant for life, her child would be the same when he or she was born. Slavery could be passed on from mother to child forever. All of this had happend by the year 1670.

Take John Punch. He was a servant in the early days before the term "slave" was used. He ran away with two others, and they were caught. The two others were white men, and they were whipped for running away (people were often whipped, as a punishment, until the nineteenth century) and sent back to their master. The white men were also told they had to serve their master longer than they originally had to, to make up for the time they had lost by running away. John Punch was whipped and sent back, too. But he was told that he would have to serve his master not just for a few extra months or even years, but for the rest of his life. John Punch was treated differently because he was black.

It took almost half a century after the first Africans came in 1619, but slowly black "servants" became "slaves." The word itself finally appeared in the law-books. Slavery happened because the English colonists badly needed the workers, and because they convinced themselves that these dark people who did not look like Englishmen were inferior human beings who were good only for fieldwork and for serving the white people. As slaves became more and more valuable, more were brought to America.

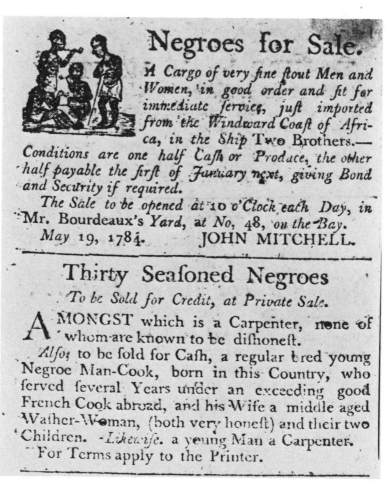

Advertising human beings for sale, just after the American Revolution.

THE BIRTH OF SLAVERY IN AMERICA

By the time Thomas Jefferson sat down to write the Declaration of Independence in 1776, slavery had been a fact in the thirteen colonies for more than a century. There were more slaves in the South because that was where the biggest farms were. These large farms, called plantations, grew tobacco, rice, some cotton and some sugar (later there would be much more cotton). Slavery was legal in every one of the colonies fighting against England in the American Revolution, and there were a few slaves even in the far North.

Didn't anyone think it was wrong? Certainly the black Africans did, but they were not able to change anything because they were just slaves. As time went on many white people began to think slavery was wrong, too, even white people who owned slaves. Benjamin Franklin did not own slaves, and as a printer he published several pamphlets saying slavery was wrong. Even Jefferson, a Virginia plantation owner and master of hundreds of slaves, did not think it right. He did not know how to solve the problem, but he looked out of the windows of his beautiful home in Virginia, a home built by slave workers, and he wrote, "I tremble for my country when I reflect that God is just; that his justice cannot sleep forever." He meant that surely God could not approve of one man owning others, like cattle, and that he would punish America for it.

But when Jefferson wrote those words there were already over one hundred thousand slaves in the United States, and more coming all the time. How they got here from their homes in Africa is one of the great tragic stories of human history.

CHAPTER 3

To Kidnap a Continent

IBRAHINA WAS TRAPPED. His cavalry troop had been ambushed on an African hillside as they returned from a successful campaign against their enemies. A prince of the Fulbe people, son of the powerful King Sori, Ibrahima did not intend to die meekly or be taken prisoner. With his men killed or run off and only a handful of his guard left, he sat on the ground holding the bridle of his horse. A short sword was concealed beneath his robes. The ambushers surrounded him and approached, guns drawn.

"I will not run," Ibrahima said quietly, and when the first of his enemies came close enough he sprang forward and killed the man. He expected to die instantly himself, but he was struck in the head with a rifle butt and fell unconscious. When he awoke he was drenched. They had thrown him into a pond to revive him. His fine clothes and sandals were gone, and his hands were tied.

Ibrahima, Prince of the Fulbe of West Africa, was beginning a terrifying journey to the New World as a slave. The year was 1788, the same year the United States adopted its Constitution and first elected George Washington president.

A slave "factory" on the African coast, where Africans
were sold for shipment to America, about 1730.

What happened to Ibrahima next happened to millions
of Africans in the sixteenth, seventeenth, and eighteenth
centuries. West Africa, below the vast Sahara Desert and
above the rain forest of the Congo Basin, had been a
land of great kingdoms and extensive culture. But there
had been warfare, too, much like that in Europe, and
captives were often kept as slaves by the conquerors. The
local slavery of West Africa, however, at least took place
among people who were fairly similar. Slavery is never
kind, but it is less terrible when the slave stays in a place
he knows and works for people who understand him. In
West Africa slaves were usually protected by law or

23

custom, and they sometimes gained freedom and a new life among their captors. Then the Europeans began coming to Africa, looking for slaves to carry far away to the New World. The slaves they took would have to work very hard, and the Europeans did not care very much what happened to them. The Europeans could harden their hearts against these strange African people whose world the whites neither understood nor appreciated.

Ibrahima was marched barefoot over a hundred miles to the coast to a trading center on the banks of the Gambia River. Whole gangs were often driven to the coast, as one observer said, "in large bodies, tied together by the neck." Ibrahima was purchased by an English sea captain named Nevin, and immediately he had iron bands locked on his wrists and ankles. With nearly 170 other captured Africans he was crowded below the deck of the slave ship *Africa*. He had been sold, and would be sold again in the New World. He was a slave, and he could never expect to see his homeland or his family again.

Ibrahima was educated in several African languages, and he knew what was happening to him all the while, for he could understand what was said around him. Perhaps that was less frightening than being one of the many less-educated captives who had no idea what was to become of them. Or, maybe knowing made it worse.

Olaudah Equiano was one of those who had never even seen the ocean, or any white people, and when he was sold in 1756 he had no idea what the future held in store. He wrote later:

TO KIDNAP A CONTINENT

The first object which saluted my eyes when I arrived on the coast was the sea, and a slave ship, which was then riding at anchor, and waiting for its cargo. These filled me with astonishment, which was soon converted into terror. . . . I was persuaded that I had got into a world of bad spirits, and that they were going to kill me.

As he looked in horror around the ship he saw "a multitude of black people of every description chained together, every one . . . expressing dejection and sorrow." He fainted.

The passage of the slave ships to America was almost too horrible to believe. The ships tried to carry as many people as they could possibly crowd in, and no one worried about the comfort, safety, or health of the slaves. They were kept on cramped shelves, lying down, often with their feet chained to the ship's hull so they could not leave their place. The decks were built especially close together in slave ships. You could not stand in the three- or four-foot high chambers, but had to crawl to get in and out. If the weather were good, the crew might let the slaves out on deck, a few at a time, to get fresh air and exercise. Then they were returned to the stinking hold below deck.

Sickness was automatic in such conditions. A captain figured he had a good trip if no more than one out of every ten people in his human "cargo" died on the westward crossing of the Atlantic. The trip took weeks even in good weather. Those who died were simply thrown overboard so they would not infect the other slaves with their sickness. It was said that sharks used to follow the slave ships. One English navy captain, disgusted by the slave trade, said that if the wind were blowing in the right direction you could smell a slave ship before you could see it.

Added to all this misery was the terror of not knowing where you were going, or what would become of you.

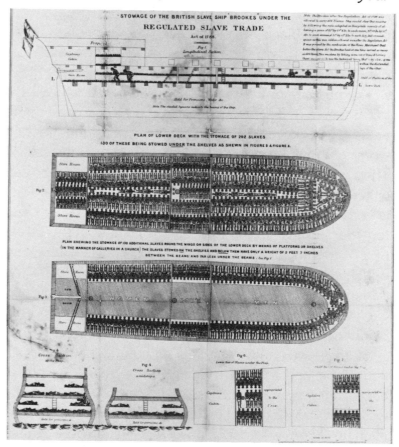

How slaves crossed the Atlantic: a cutaway view of the British slave ship, *Brookes,* late eighteenth century.

TO KIDNAP A CONTINENT

Across the Atlantic at last, slaves were sold to plantation owners or, more often, to slave dealers who bought them in large groups for resale to the planters who could not come to the seacoast. Slaves were sold right off the ship or taken ashore to be inspected like livestock by the buyers. Slave traders would look at their height, weight, and how strong they were. They would peer into the slaves' mouths to check their teeth. Most of the slaves were young men, strong workers who would bring a high price. But some were women, and some merely children. Buyers did not care about families or friends. They just bought individual slaves with little thought of keeping people together. There were several brothers on Equiano's ship who were all bought by different traders. They never saw each other again, though they pleaded with the traders to be kept together.

Many slaves stopped first in the islands of the Caribbean before coming to mainland America. Ibrahima was one of these. At the tiny island of Dominica he was purchased from Nevin by a trader named John Irwin. Irwin was one of those men who made their living buying and selling slaves.

Ibrahima's and Olaudah Equiano's stories were just two out of millions. From the time the first African "servants" arrived in Virginia in 1619 until the American Civil War in the early 1860s, a time of nearly two and a half centuries, Africans in huge numbers were brought to North America against their will to work in the fields.

The cruelty of the slave trade is difficult to understand. It was a terrible business, but it was just that—a business. The African dealers, the Europeans of many nations who

27

ran the trading forts (called factories) on the coast, the ships' captains, the dealers in the New World—all of these people bought and sold human beings without regard for their feelings or their rights or their basic human dignity. They did it for the money; it was as simple as that.

Finally, the civilized nations of the world began to outlaw the slave trade, and tried to stop it on the high seas with their navies. The United States made it illegal to import slaves after 1808 (though slavery itself was still legal in the South). But such was the profit to be made, and so high was the demand for slaves to work in the cotton fields, that slaves were smuggled into the country against the law. The U.S. navy in the nineteenth century was too tiny to stop the slave trade. In a busy year, as many as 10,000 Africans were brought into the United States illegally.

In the centuries in which the slave trade operated, Africa was robbed of millions of her people. These kidnapped Africans brought their lives, their labor and their culture to help make America what it is today.

CHAPTER 4

Work Never Done

WHEN THE ENGLISH settled Jamestown, North America was a wilderness. By the time slavery was ended, the wilderness was pushed back west of the Mississippi River and the United States bustled with farms and cities. Much of the work that made that happen was done by slaves. And that was the most constant thing in the life of a slave—work.

They cleared land. They planted. They weeded. They picked the crop and cleaned it and sent it off to market. They cared for the animals, built and repaired buildings, plowed and cooked and sewed. That's why they were there in the first place, and slave owners sometimes went to a lot of trouble and even cruelty to make sure that the slaves did, indeed, work hard. Much of America, especially in the South, was built by slaves.

Solomon Northrup was a slave in the 1840s. He had been free and living in the North, but he was kidnapped and spent twelve years in slavery before he was found and set free. He remembered his work, and his experience was a lot like what other slaves went through.

He worked with cotton most of the time. Cotton grows on a bushlike plant that grows about as high as a man.

CAPTIVE BODIES, FREE SPIRITS

The seeds of the cotton plant are found in a puffy round cluster called a boll. What protects the seeds and makes the boll puffy is a fuzzy white plant fiber, and that is what makes cotton valuable. Those fuzzy white fibers could be cleaned and spun into thread, and the thread woven into cloth. Cotton cloth is one of the most useful and popular fabrics in the world. The problem is that it takes a warm climate to grow cotton, and lots of work, too. The American South had the climate. The slaves did the work.

Northrup remembered plowing for cotton in March or early April. Oxen and mules pulled the plow, making deep furrows across the field six feet apart. Down the middle of the space between the furrows they made another slit for planting the seed. A slave would plant the seed from a bag hung around his neck. On Northrup's plantation, this job was done by a girl. Then the plow would cover up the seed. After planting, the slaves went with hoes to the cotton fields to thin out the plants, leaving only the biggest, and clear away the weeds. They would march through the fields in a bunch, while someone on horseback watched to keep them working. If anyone slowed up or didn't work as fast as the others, the master or the foreman would hit him with a whip.

On Northrup's plantation, the fastest man with a hoe was put on the first row and given a head start. If anyone hoed fast enough on another row to pass the first man, the first man was whipped for being lazy.

Caring for the growing cotton crop went on most of the summer. By late August, it was time to pick the cotton bolls. Northrup was given a burlap sack to put around his neck. It reached from his chest all the way to the ground.

WORK NEVER DONE

With this he was sent down the rows of cotton, picking as fast as he could, putting the cotton into his sack. When the sack was full, he dumped it into a basket at the end of the row. At sundown the master weighed the cotton each slave had picked and if the weight was less than the master thought it should be, the slave was punished. The master knew who the best pickers were, and they were expected to bring home the most. Cotton bolls are light, but Northrup's master expected at least two hundred pounds a day from even the slowest of his slaves.

The fastest picker on Northrup's plantation was a woman, "Patsey . . . (was) the most remarkable cotton picker on Bayou Boeuf," he remembered. "She picked with both hands and with such surprising rapidity, that five hundred pounds a day was not unusual for her." But instead of being rewarded for her speed, Patsey was just expected to do more every day or get a whipping for being lazy.

After the cotton was picked, it had to be cleaned and "ginned" (that is, the seeds removed from the fibers by a machine called a cotton gin) and pressed into big rectangular blocks called bales. Then there was other farm work. Hogs had to be slaughtered and cleaned and cured into pork and ham. Food crops, like corn and potatoes, needed tending. Fences were repaired, new land cleared. There were changes from season to season, but there was never any shortage of work.

The day began before dawn on most plantations. Some owners rang a bell, some blew a horn. Solomon Northrup had to be in the field by the time it was light. At midday he was given about fifteen minutes to eat a lunch of cold bacon that was brought to him out in the field. Then it was back to work until it was too dark to see. Because growing cotton required daylight, the work days were longer in summer, shorter in winter. But when work was heavy at harvest time, a bright full moon meant that slaves could work well into the night.

On plantations where they grew sugar cane, the hardest time of the year was from the middle of October until almost Christmas. That was when the cane was cut. The slaves hurried to beat the first frost of the winter. Then, before it rotted, the cane had to be taken to a kind of factory, where the long stalks were crushed. During these frantic weeks, slaves worked sixteen to eighteen hours a day, seven days a week.

Rice plantations meant a different kind of work. Rice grows in fields covered by water, and in addition to their other chores, the slaves had to learn to operate floodgates to let the rivers flow in and out of the fields.

Most slaves worked in large groups on big plantations. Others were owned by small farmers who had only a slave or two. These small farmers often worked right alongside their slaves, because they could not afford to be idle and leave it all up to the slaves.

As Ibrahima stood in the slave lot in Natchez, after his journey from Africa, he was inspected carefully by a man named Thomas Foster. Foster bought Ibrahima and another slave for $930.00. The farmer had not been on the Mississippi frontier very long; no one had. It was a new, raw settlement and most of the farmers were still poor and owned very few acres. Foster led his two new slaves through the forest to his small tobacco farm in a five-acre clearing surrounded by a fence.

For his first job, Ibrahima, once a proud prince, carried tobacco that had been cut by a more experienced slave. He knew about tobacco, since it was grown in his home country. But Ibrahima had never personally worked with it. The hardest part of the work was transplanting the young plants by hand into straight rows. This job was done in the rain, if possible, when the dirt was soft. It was hard work, done on hands and knees, and Master Foster probably did it, too. Like cotton, tobacco was hoed to keep down weeds. Bugs were picked off by hand, because they had no such thing as insecticide in those days. Then, at harvest, the tobacco leaves were cut and dried and packed into huge barrels for shipment. In his first year on Foster's farm, Ibrahima helped to raise eight thousand pounds of tobacco under the hot Mississippi sun.

After a few years, Foster switched from tobacco to cotton, and Ibrahima and the three other slaves Foster now owned learned cotton farming. The routine was similar to that which Solomon Northrup knew, but working conditions were different because Northrup was on a large plantation with many slaves while Ibrahima worked on a small farm. Northrup hardly knew the person who owned him. Ibrahima lived and worked beside his owner every day. The thing which both slaves shared was the common ingredient of all slavery, work itself.

If you were a slave, how hard you had to work

depended on a lot of things—the kind of crop you grew, the kind of job you had, the season of the year, and who owned you. Sometimes owners pushed their slaves without mercy, making them work very hard all the time. Some owners were easier on their slaves, either because they were kind or because they believed that in the long run the results were better if the slaves were not half dead from overwork. Sometimes the worst situation was to be under a man called an overseer. An overseer worked for the master. He was a kind of foreman whose job it was to keep after the slaves. Very often the overseer himself was under a lot of pressure from the plantation owner to make a lot of money. Then he would drive the slaves hard, not caring what happened to them. Most slaves agreed that the worst thing was to be worked by a bad overseer.

Sometimes another slave was put in charge of the work gangs. Such a person was called a driver, because his job was to drive the slaves across the field to do their work, using his whip if necessary.

Slaves, of course, did not get paid. They got a place to live, clothes, and food. Their homes were usually just dirt-floored shacks somewhere out behind the master's house. The clothes were cheap, usually jeans or rough wool pants, rough shirts, and maybe shoes. Children usually had a long shirt, like a nightshirt, and nothing else. The food was just as simple and cheap. Slaves got flour, cornmeal, some potatoes, some molasses, and some meat, usually bacon or salted pork. It was a poor diet, and not much to go on when you had so much work to do.

WORK NEVER DONE

Unless it was harvest time, or some other emergency, slaves usually got Sunday off, and sometimes part of Saturday. Most slaves got a longer break at lunch than Solomon Northrup remembered. When it was really hot the master might give them an hour or two at midday to rest. Then again, he might not. Some slaves used their free time to grow a garden, if the master let them. This garden not only gave them some rare fresh vegetables for their diet, but some personal satisfaction as well. At least here they were creating something for themselves.

Some masters let their slaves have a holiday now and then, especially at Christmas. The slaves would receive presents like bandanas, or tobacco, or some other treat. One year one rice planter gave each of his slaves twelve quarts of rice, one quart of molasses, two pipes, and some tobacco. Hats and cloth for dresses were popular gifts. Sometimes gifts were not just for Christmas, but rewards for good behavior and good work. That was the only way an average slave got "paid."

Some slaves did earn money. The master might let them grow a garden and sell their produce in town. Ibrahima did this, with Foster's permission. Other slaves were "hired out," as Henry Brown was. That is, one man would pay Brown's master for the use of Brown at his factory. It was like renting a human being. Henry Brown got a little of the money to keep for himself.

Not all the slave workers were men. Women often worked hard in the fields, too. Some women were house servants, and their lives were somewhat easier, or at least spent in more elegant surroundings. Cooks were usually women, but in the days of country kitchens, being the cook for a whole farm or plantation was not easy. The cook had to get up early to prepare breakfast, and ended the day, after cleaning up from dinner, by going to the woods for firewood for the next day.

Even the children worked. By age six they were big enough to haul water to the field hands, or to tag along after their mother to help her with her chores. By the time a slave child was ten or twelve years old, he was put to regular work, although not as much was expected of him as of an adult. A slave was considered grown up by seventeen or eighteen.

Some slaves learned special jobs around the farm or plantation. A plantation was usually fairly isolated from town, and people who lived on one had to take care of most things themselves. Some slaves became expert carpenters or blacksmiths. Henry Brown learned to mix tobacco and went to live in a town to do his job. Simon Gray was a slave who ran a Mississippi River flatboat, carrying goods between Natchez and New Orleans around the year 1850. He could move about pretty much as he wished and was boss of a crew of ten to twenty other men. His master trusted him, and all Simon Gray had to do was report now and then on how he was doing.

By the time the American Civil War broke out, there were almost four million slaves in the United States. They lived in the South, because by then slavery was not legal in the North. Four million people, four million stories. Not one slave lived exactly the same life as any other slave. Each one had his own master, his own personality, his

WORK NEVER DONE

own sorrow and joy. They all worked, one way or another, whether it was because they wanted to or because they were afraid of the master's whip. But even for a slave, there was life outside of work. They tried to take those few moments and make the most of them.

CHAPTER 5

Families in Fear

MARY REYNOLDS WAS old, nearly one hundred years old. She sat talking to the young man who had come to interview her. Slavery was a long time gone, and there were very few people left who had lived as a slave and remembered it. Mary Reynolds remembered, and she told the young man about it. Like all slave stories, hers is unique because each person is unique. But Mary Reynolds's story says a lot about life as a slave.

Her father's name was Tom Vaughn, and he was free, not a slave, even though he was black. He had lived in the North, and built and tuned pianos for a living. Work must have been scarce, because when some white people asked him to come South to do his work, he went, even though the South was the land of slavery.

He met Mary's mother in Louisiana. She was a slave, and her first husband had died. Tom wanted to marry her. Since a slave was someone's property, he or she could not marry without the master's permission. Tom tried to buy the woman from her master. He would not sell her. All that Tom could do, if he wanted to marry the slave woman, was to go to work for the same master, and that is what he did. Whether he, too, became a slave, or

FAMILIES IN FEAR

just worked for his room and board, or pay, Mary did not say. Maybe she never knew. Tom and his wife (we do not know her name) had six children, including Mary.

Mary was born at the same time as Dora, the master's daughter. Dora's mother died giving birth, and Mary's mother took care of the white baby. It was not unusual for slave women, especially those with babies of their own, to help raise white children. Mary and Dora played together when they were very small and became best friends.

Then the master, Dora's father, sold Mary to a white man in town. Mary didn't remember how old she was, just that she "was just 'bout big 'nough to start playing with a broom to go 'bout sweeping up and not even half doing it." Dora was so upset at losing her only playmate that she actually got sick, or so it seemed. The doctor advised her father to buy Mary back in order to help Dora get well. The man did, and sure enough, Dora recovered.

But as Dora got older, she began to have schooling and other white playmates. Her father remarried, and the new mistress of the plantation had children of her own by her first husband. Dora played with them. Mary was left down in the slave quarters with the other black children.

Mary started working as a child, hoeing corn at first. An old slave woman tried to teach her and the other children, but little Mary kept knocking down the corn along with the weeds. The old woman told her she'd better learn to do it right or the driver, named Solomon, would punish her. All of her life as a slave Mary would know the fear that if she did wrong, or angered the master, she would be punished. Most slaves lived with that fear. Punishment usually meant being whipped. At least once Mary got a dreadful whipping, so severe it nearly killed her. As an old woman she remembered it bitterly.

Mary lived in the slave cabins with her parents and brothers and sisters. Her cabin was better than the average. "It was nice and warm," she remembered. It was made of pine boards and had a fireplace. Many slave quarters did not have a fireplace. The beds in Mary's cabin were boards attached to the wall, covered with a mattress stuffed with shucks, the stiff leaves taken off ears of corn. At night the men would sometimes find the time and material to make chairs for the cabins. That was all the furniture Mary remembered.

They had a garden patch behind the cabins. Potatoes were the thing Mary liked best. "Taters roasted in the ashes was the best-tasting eating I ever had," she said. Her master would let the slaves sell extra vegetables from their garden in town. They had to have a special pass from the master to go, and they had to go at night after the work was done.

Saturday night and Sunday were free time. Clothes were washed in the creek on Saturday night and hung in the woods to dry. Saturday night was also the time for partying. On cold nights the slaves would make an outdoor fire. All the entertainment had to be homemade, so they would sing, dance, and play any musical instruments they had. The instruments, like fiddles and guitars and banjos, were either homemade or gifts from the master or bought with money earned in town selling produce from the garden. In fact, "banjo" is an African word brought to America by the black people.

Mary's master did not care much about getting his slaves to church on Sunday. Many masters were very serious about church, and thought that one of the best things they could do was teach these Africans about Christianity. Some masters took their slaves to church with them, where the slaves usually sat in their own special section in the back of the church or up in the balcony, apart from the whites. Some masters had a preacher come and hold services for the slaves right on the farm. Other masters would try to do the job themselves by reading the Bible to their slaves. Often the slaves would hold their own "church," praying, singing, and reading the Bible, if anyone among them had been taught to read.

Mary's family and their friends would pray in their cabins and sing softly. They tried to be quiet because Solomon, the slave driver, didn't like the slaves to be together like that. It seemed to make him nervous, and if he heard them praying and singing he would bang on the cabin wall with his whip handle and threaten them if they did not stop.

Religion was quite important for many of the slaves. What they learned from the Bible was that God looked at all people alike, black or white, and that all humans would get a chance to be in Heaven if they were good. The Bible told slaves that this life is just a short time on the way to everlasting life in Heaven. This idea kept the slaves' spirits up when life got hard.

CAPTIVE BODIES, FREE SPIRITS

The masters figured that it was fine for slaves to think this way, because the slaves would not get so desperate about how bad life could be. When white people taught religion to slaves, the parts of the Bible they used most were the ones that told people to be patient and wait for Heaven, and to obey their masters while on earth.

Some churches developed special catechisms, or lessons, for slaves to memorize. A slave catechism from the year 1854 went:

Q. Who keeps the snakes and all bad things from hurting you?
A. God does.

Q. Who gave you a master and a mistress?
A. God gave them to me.

Q. Who says that you must obey them?
A. God says that I must.

Q. What book tells you these things?
A. The Bible.

Q. How does God do all his work?
A. He always does it right.

Q. Does God love to work?
A. Yes, God is always at work.

Q. Do the angels work?
A. Yes, they do what God tells them.

Q. Do they love to work?
A. Yes, they love to please God.

Q. What does God say about your work?
A. He that will not work shall not eat.

Q. Did Adam and Eve have to work?
A. Yes, they had to keep the garden.

Q. Was it hard to keep that garden?

A. No, it was very easy.

Q. What makes the crops so hard to grow now?

A. Sin makes it.

Q. What makes you lazy?

A. My wicked heart.

Q. How do you know your heart is wicked?

A. I feel it every day.

Q. Who teaches you so many wicked things?

A. The Devil.

Q. Must you let the Devil teach you?

A. No, I must not.

Once Mary's parents took her and her sister Katherine off the plantation without permission to hear a black preacher somewhere nearby. They slipped away in the dark, risking a whipping or worse. At the prayer meeting an old black man with a white beard told Mary and the others that the day was coming when they would be servants only to God. They all prayed, Mary remembered, "for the end of tribulation and the end of beatings and for shoes that fit our feet. We prayed that . . . (we) could have all we wanted to eat and special for fresh meat." Then, when the meeting was over and they began to walk back home in the dark, they heard the dogs.

"Maw," Mary cried, "it's them hounds!" The patrol was out with tracking dogs, trying to find slaves who were away without permission.

"Sure 'nough," Mary's mother said in fear, "them dogs am running and God help us!"

CAPTIVE BODIES, FREE SPIRITS

Mary and her sister were hidden in a fence corner by their parents and told not to move, no matter what. Then the parents took off through the woods, trying to draw the dogs away. The two little girls stood terrified, holding hands and too scared to breathe deeply for fear of being heard. The dogs came nearer and nearer—and then passed by. Their mother's trick worked, and the hounds went off into the woods. The little girls ran back to the cabin, and shortly after, their parents made it home the back way, eluding the dogs. Mary's mother said it was the power of God on their side.

When the first Africans were brought to the United States, they learned about the Christian religion from their masters. Christianity was not known in West Africa, where the slaves had come from, until the Europeans brought it. The slave trade and Christianity came to this part of Africa together. Native African religions—and there were many of them—were different from Christianity. Instead of one God, there were many. These deities were associated with nature, like the gods and goddesses of the sun, moon, rain, and earth.

African cultures also worshipped the family's ancestors. Family and tribal lands were important to Africans, partly because the sacred ancestors were buried there and because the tribal gods were part of the land. It was very hard on Africans to be torn away from their homes to become slaves in the new world. It was hard, too, to come from a culture where families were so important, and then have no right to keep your family together. By the time Mary Reynolds was a child, in the middle of the nineteenth century, Christianity had mostly replaced the

44

FAMILIES IN FEAR

African religions. But sometimes in slave superstitions, or in the belief of natural spirits and magic, traces of the old ways could still be seen in the Christian slaves.

When the slaves could sing their own religious songs, they showed that they saw different things in the Bible than their white owners did. Black spirituals told of mercy in Heaven, and how God would deliver oppressed people from captivity. One favorite spiritual was based on the Old Testament story of Moses leading the Israelites out of Egypt.

> When Israel was in Egypt's land,
> Let my people go.
> Oppressed so hard they could not stand,
> Let my people go.
> Thus spoke the Lord, bold Moses said,
> Let my people go.
> If not I'll smite your first-born dead
> Let my people go.
>
> Go down, Moses,
> 'Way down in Egypt's land,
> Tell ole Pharaoh,
> To let my people go.

Their songs spoke a lot about judgment day, when all would be equal and they would be taken to Heaven.

> He delivered Daniel from the lion's den,
> Jonah from the belly of the whale,
> An' the Hebrew children from the fiery furnace,
> An' why not every man.

CAPTIVE BODIES, FREE SPIRITS

Didn't my Lord deliver Daniel
  deliver Daniel, deliver Daniel.
Didn't my Lord deliver Daniel,
An' why not every man.

And they sang about freedom.

    Way down yonder in the graveyard walk,
    I thank God I'm free at last,
    Me and Jesus gonna meet and talk,
    I thank God I'm free at last.

    One of these mornins bright and fair,
    I thank God I'm free at last,
    Gonna meet my Jesus in the middle o' the air,
    I thank God I'm free at last.

    Free at last, free at last,
    I thank God I'm free at last,
    Free at last, free at last,
    I thank God I'm free at last.

In these spirituals, the slaves not only found their own message in the Bible, they also sang it in their own special way. Slave songs were a lot like the songs of Africa, and the style had been passed down from parents to children over the many years that black people had been in America. These songs often repeated lines, for example, in a pattern called "shout and response." A leader would sing one line, and the rest would sing the next, responding to him. This was an old African musical pattern.

Sometimes slaves at work in the field would sing to

break the monotony and to keep up a kind of rhythm. Whites listening to the singing slaves would often think that they were happy at their work. But Frederick Douglass, an escaped slave and leader in the fight against slavery, knew better. He said:

> I have often been utterly astonished, since I came to the north, to find persons who could speak of the singing, among slaves, as evidence of their contentment and happiness. It is impossible to conceive of a greater mistake. Slaves sing most when they are most unhappy. The songs of the slave represent the sorrows of his heart; and he is relieved by them, only as an aching heart is relieved by its tears.

When Mary Reynolds was grown, she was ready to take a husband. She wanted to marry one of the other slaves on the plantation. Her master had to give permission, and he did. A slave marriage was not usually treated like a marriage for whites. Mary and her groom just stood outside the cabin door, and a broom handle was held low across the opening. The owner and his wife were there, and the mistress put a wreath on Mary's head. Then Mary and her husband stepped over the broom into the cabin, and that was it. They were called married. Later, after the Civil War when she was free, Mary Reynolds went to a church for a real wedding, and had her name and her husband's put properly into the church records.

When Ibrahima had been working for Thomas Foster for several years, Foster bought a woman slave and a few children. The woman was probably mother to the children, but the records are not clear and we do not know for sure. Isabella was her name, and she was born in the United States, not in Africa. She had lived in South Carolina and had been brought to Mississippi by her former owner, who sold her to Foster.

A few months after she came to the Fosters' farm, Isabella and Ibrahima were married. Foster was a religious man, and unlike Mary Reynolds's master, he arranged for a proper wedding, on Christmas Day, 1794. After the ceremony, Foster and the slaves celebrated with a wedding feast, with fresh roasted meat and brandy. For Ibrahima, marriage meant that he had finally accepted his life in the New World, and knew he would never go home to Africa, where he already had a wife. In the six years after they were married, Isabella and Ibrahima had three children.

The slave family was as important to its members as any family, but family life was not always possible for slaves. Slaves were property. They could not control their own lives. They could be moved, sold, traded, or handled however the master wanted. Husbands could not protect wives. Mothers could not be sure their children would not be sold. Parents could not protect their children from being whipped if the master chose to whip them. Marriages, as Mary Reynolds's story shows, were often not taken seriously. Families had no right to stay together.

Slave families could not even control the names of their children unless the master let them. Naming slaves was often left to the owner. The African names of newly arrived slaves were too complicated to pronounce, or

A drawing of a slave auction in the South, early 1861.
Note the seven-star Confederate flag in the background.

sounded heathen to the whites. The masters called the
slaves by westernized names, like John or Mary, or
sometimes gave them mockingly fancy, classical Latin
names, like Caesar or Pompey. This renaming was
another way to break the slaves' connection to Africa and
to get them to accept their new life in bondage in
America. Thomas Foster could have called Ibrahima,
Abraham, because that would have been a literal transla-
tion of the slave's name. Instead, Foster nicknamed
Ibrahima, "Prince," because Foster was amused that the
slave kept saying he used to be a prince in his own
country.

In modern America, some black people are changing
their names to get rid of what they call the old slave

names. Those who join various branches of the Islamic religion commonly do this. Muhammad Ali (formerly Cassius Clay) and Kareem Abdul Jabbar (Lew Alcindor) are famous examples of this.

Josiah Henson was just a little boy in Montgomery County, Maryland, when his own family was torn apart because the master died, and his estate, including his slaves, was sold off at an auction. The slaves were taken to the front of the crowd and sold to the highest bidder, one at a time. One by one Henson's brothers and sisters were sold to different people, "while my mother, paralyzed by grief, held me by the hand," he remembered. "Her turn came, and she was bought by Isaac Riley of Montgomery County. Then I was offered to the assembled purchasers. My mother, half distracted with the thought of parting forever from all her children, pushed through the crowd . . . to the spot where Riley was standing. She fell at his feet, and clung to his knees," begging the man to buy her little boy so that at least one of her children could stay with her. Angrily, the man kicked her repeatedly until she had to crawl away, weeping, to get away from his blows. "I must have been then between five and six years old," Josiah Henson wrote years later, but "I seem to see and hear my poor weeping mother now."

Not all slaves had to endure such misery. Many were able to stay most of their life in one place, with one family of owners. Even if they were moved or sold, some were able to stay with their family. Sometimes a new owner would buy an entire family, even if all he really wanted was the one slave. The problem was that the way families were treated depended on the kindness and wealth of the master. Families had no rights of their own, for slaves were property. Property does not have legal rights; property owners do. The threat of separation was always there. An Englishman who saw slaves traded in the United States said, "So long as the slave trade continues there can be no sense of security for the slave, and without security it is a mockery to talk of happiness."

We know from all the historical records that slaves were bought, sold, and moved all the time. Some people made a living being slave traders, like John Irwin, who sold Ibrahima to Thomas Foster. What must it have been like to be in a business that bought and sold people? What must it have been like to be bought and sold?

Slave traders were not well-respected people, for the most part. Even the people who owned and used slaves, and who used the services of the slave traders, did not like them, because it was such a cruel business. Yet many people became wealthy by moving people around and selling them.

In the autumn of 1834, a man named George Featherstonhaugh saw a typical slave march. Three hundred slaves were being taken from Virginia to a slave sale down in Natchez, Mississippi, the same place where Ibrahima had been sold many years before. (Slaves often went from the upper and eastern parts of the South— Virginia, Maryland, North Carolina—to the southern and western states. That was because the old plantation regions were worn out after centuries of farming, and people were moving to new places and taking their need for slave workers with them.) Featherstonhaugh saw the

Slaves on the march to the deep South.

slaves as they were waking up after having spent the night camping in the woods. The women and children were free to move about, but all the men were tied together with chains. They even slept that way. This was to prevent them from running away. The white men who were in charge were well dressed, and stood by laughing and smoking cigars.

As Featherstonhaugh watched, the slaves broke camp and crossed the river, the men by wading through the swift current, the women and children on rafts or wagons. The slave traders watched with great care, Featherstonhaugh noted, and later he learned that near that very spot, only a few months earlier, a similar traveling gang had broken free, killed the white traders with axes, and run away.

FAMILIES IN FEAR

At the end of the march was the slave market. Most of the major cities of the South had dealers with their own places to keep and sell slaves. Sometimes there was a public slave auction, right in the town square. Joseph Ingraham accompanied his white friend, who wanted to buy a slave, to a market in Natchez, perhaps the very same one the Virginia slaves were bound for. Forty black men stood on one side, arranged in a line from the tallest down to the shortest, a little boy of about ten. On the other side was a line of about twenty women. The slaves were all neatly dressed for sale; they even had hats.

Ingraham's friend looked them all over, and then the dealer came up. "Good morning, gentlemen!" he said cheerily, "Would you like to examine my lot of boys? I have as fine a lot as ever came into market." Ingraham's friend said he needed a coachman. The dealer asked a slave named George to step forward. George said he was from Virginia, and had driven his mistress's coach for four years. The buyer asked George if he had a good appetite, if he were even-tempered or easily angered, and other questions. George said his age was about twenty-three, but he wasn't sure. He had been married in Virginia, but now he had a "new wife" from among the group that had been brought to Mississippi for sale.

After haggling a bit on the price, the dealer sold George to Ingraham's friend for $950.00. At the pleading of his new slave, the owner also bought Jane, George's new wife, as a seamstress, for $750.00, but with a provision that he could return her if she didn't work out.

Sometimes instead of being simply sold, slaves were auctioned. A slave would be brought before a crowd and

53

an auctioneer would get the prospective buyers to keep bidding higher and higher until the slave was sold.

Frederika Bremer, traveling in this country in 1850, saw an auction in New Orleans. It was held in a large basement, with the sound of heavy rain beating on the walls and windows. The auctioneer was a hearty, cheerful man, who looked, Bremer said, as if he had just come from eating a good breakfast. One of the first slaves for sale was a tall, "noble-looking" young woman wearing a gray dress and a yellow scarf on her head. She held an infant child in her arms. Standing on the auction table for everyone to inspect and consider, she kept her head down and did not move. She seemed to see nothing but her baby. She and the child were to be sold together.

The auctioneer began to tell of her good qualities—her intelligence, good disposition, domestic skills, religious nature. He even noted that her value was increased by the child who came with her as a kind of bonus. The bidding got to $500.00. "Gentlemen," pleaded the auctioneer, "I am offered $500.00 for this superior woman and her child. It is not a sum to be thought of! She, with her child, is worth double that money!" In the end she brought a price of $700.00. She stepped down and waited silently at the side of the room while the auction went on. There is no way to know what became of her.

Slave families had reason to fear the slave traders. Even the best master might get into debt or have financial troubles that forced him or her to sell off the slaves, and there was no guarantee at all that families would be kept together. The woman Frederika Bremer saw was sold because her master had guaranteed another man's debt and had to pay up when the debtor skipped town. And, of course, not all masters could be trusted, as a slave named Manuel found out.

Manuel and his family belonged to a man we know only as Mr. G——. Manuel lived in Washington, DC, a slave in the capital of the United States. There he met the same George Featherstonhaugh who described the slave march in Virginia. Featherstonhaugh told Manuel's story.

It was late in the afternoon, and Featherstonhaugh was eating a hasty supper as he got ready to leave for a trip. A messenger delivered a note from a woman friend of his, begging for his help. The woman knew of a slave named Manuel, who worked for Mr. G—— at a hotel in Washington. She liked Manuel, and she was worried. He had disappeared, and was rumored to be in the hands of a slave dealer near the city.

Featherstonhaugh left his meal and hastily hired a carriage to take him to the slave dealer's office. It turned out to be, he said, "neither more nor less than a jail . . . ; manacles, fetters, and all sorts of offensive things were lying about." The superintendent was a hard-looking man, clearly little more than a jailkeeper. "Where is a slave named Manuel?" Featherstonhaugh asked. The superintendent picked up a heavy key and unlocked a huge door that was also fastened with chains and bars. Behind it was a large room full of black men; one of them was Manuel.

Featherstonhaugh stepped into the slave jail and asked Manuel what had happened. Sadly, fearfully, the slave told him a tale of treachery.

CAPTIVE BODIES, FREE SPIRITS

Mr. G—— had sent Manuel to the slave dealer's with "a message," but when Manuel got there he was taken prisoner and placed in the large locked room. He was afraid he had been kidnapped. Later, when Manuel did not return, Mr. G—— sent Manuel's wife and children out to find him, and they, too, were captured and locked up.

Very angry, Featherstonhaugh demanded that they be released. Then he was told the terrible truth. Mr. G—— was behind it all. He had arranged for Manuel and his family to be sold. To avoid trouble, and to keep the slaves from running away when they learned about the sale, he had set up the situation as a trap, a way to get the slaves quietly into the hands of the dealer. He had done this sort of thing before, too.

Manuel begged Featherstonhaugh to buy him and his family, but the white man did not have that kind of money. Despite the circumstances, he also did not want to have any part of owning a slave, even to save that slave from being sold away. Luckily, Featherstonhaugh was able to make last-minute arrangements to prevent the sale of the family. Most people who learned of the trick thought that Mr. G—— was despicable for what he had done, but it was all legal. There was no protection for the slave or his family.

A slave's life turned on one important point. Slaves were people who were also property. In most states, slaves were called "chattels," an old legal term meaning personal property, property like furniture or jewelry. The laws of South Carolina called slaves "chattels personal," meaning literally "people who are property." In Louisi-

FAMILIES IN FEAR

ana, and in Kentucky until 1852, slaves were not taxed as personal property. They were legally treated as real estate!

Slaves had almost no rights, and those they had could not easily be protected. The Bill of Rights, in the Constitution of the United States, did not apply to slaves because they were not really citizens of this country. The owner's rights, however, were clear, because the law in the United States specifically protected the right to own property. Louisiana law said of masters and slaves, "the master may sell him, dispose of his person, his industry, and his labor: He [meaning the slave] can do nothing, possess nothing, nor acquire anything but what must belong to his master." That explains why, for example, slave marriages were not treated like other marriages. Legally, marriage is a contract, an agreement, between two people. Slaves were property, and property can't make a legal agreement with other property. Marriage was for regular people, not slaves.

We know that the slaves really were "regular people" whose feelings we can understand. They needed strength to survive as slaves. They got that strength from faith, and from family when they had family. They told the stories and sang the songs their ancestors knew from Africa. Without rights, without legal, economic, or political power, they relied on each other in the struggle to live.

CHAPTER 6

A Contest of Wills

IT WAS AN incredible party. There was food like few of these slaves had ever seen, and wine, and music. The crowd had gathered on Colonel Alexander's property in a large shed, and by torchlight they ate and drank and danced as never before. The house servants made the finest spectacle, wearing cast-off clothes from their master or mistress. The field hands had to make do with their usual work clothes. But it didn't matter—it was the grandest party ever.

Colonel Alexander's slaves had organized it, and for weeks the word had passed around the Virginia country-side, slave to slave, plantation to plantation. Food had been "collected" all the while; that is, whenever a chicken, or even a bottle of wine, or some pork could be taken from the plantation kitchens, it was. The slaves hardly thought of this as stealing, for as one of them said, we belong to master, the food belongs to master, it's all the same thing.

The laughter, the music, the relief from their daily lives was so great that the partying slaves forgot for a time the danger. Slaves were not allowed to gather like that, without permission or supervision by white people. Many had traveled through the night from their own plantation without a pass, which was illegal. They would be whipped if caught, and they knew it, but for now the party was the thing.

Then, in mid-step, the dancers stopped, frozen in fear. The music ceased instantly. Then they heard it again, the voice of the lookout. "The patrol!"

Panic spread through the party. The slaveowners' patrol was coming! They would all be caught and punished. Some might escape, but there was no hiding the party, no denying what had gone on. They were trapped, and the horsemen were galloping closer and closer.

One of the slaves, Robert, stepped forward. He clenched his fist, and told the slaves it was impossible for all of them to get away. They must stand and fight. The terrified women were sent quickly to a nearby cabin where they hid in the dark. The lights in the shed were extinguished. A few people too frightened to stay were allowed to sneak off and find their way home as best they could. The rest of the gathering waited silently behind the closed door as the patrol came to a stop outside the barn and considered what to do.

Some patrolmen were afraid to enter the dark building; it was after midnight, and the slaves had been drinking. Who knew what desperate thing they might do? But the patrol leader was not worried. He checked his pistol, took up his cowhide whip, and told the men to follow him. "What," he said, "are you so chicken-hearted as to suppose those . . . cowardly niggers are going to get up an insurrection?" The men followed him to the door, and finding it locked, they kicked it off its hinges and strode into the blackness of the barn.

The leader was wrong. The slaves were not cowardly, and though unarmed, they would not give up this night. Barehanded, they attacked the patrol.

The battle in the dark was brief and bloody. Two members of the patrol were killed almost at once. Gunshots echoed in the barn. The flash from the pistols lit up the fight for an awful instant. A third patrolman fell with his arm broken. According to the slaves' plan, one group of them immediately slipped out the door, killed the white man holding the horses, and cut the bridles so the patrol could not ride for reinforcements and spread the alarm. A fourth white man was wounded, and then died. But the slaves were up against guns. Soon the fight was over.

Many of the survivors managed to escape, but six slaves lay dead. Robert was one of them. He left a wife and five children.

Colonel Alexander was grief-stricken at what happened. For although he did not know of the slaves' party and would not have permitted it, he did not think they had done anything so terribly wrong. His neighbors, many of whom served on the voluntary slave patrol, were angry with him. He saw to the Christian burial of his dead slaves, nonetheless, and refused to let the patrolmen come onto his property to arrest the others who might have been involved.

The tragedy at this Virginia plantation, which took place shortly after the year 1800, while Thomas Jefferson was president, was only one very dramatic incident in the ongoing battle between masters and slaves. Most of the time most slaves accepted their fate and tried to do their best. Even a slave could have pride in his work and his conduct. But from the beginning of slavery to the end, slaves kept up a steady resistance to their masters. The history of plantation slavery in America is, in part, a story of the contest of wills between the slaveowners and the people who would never totally cooperate, never totally submit.

The patrols were solid evidence of trouble. All slave states had them, and although sometimes they would be inactive for a while, hints of unrest would start them up again. Their job was to ride the countryside looking for runaways, or just slaves off their plantation without a pass. Clearly, the slaveowners were afraid of the slaves and what they might be up to.

For their part, the slaves became very skillful at hiding their feelings most of the time. It was how they survived. By appearing dumb, or happy, or confused, or indifferent, they could escape the white man's suspicions and make life easier for themselves. Time and again, owners were surprised when a slave they thought was perfectly content committed a crime or ran away. The leader of a large slave rebellion in Charleston, South Carolina, in 1822, almost wasn't caught because no one could believe that he could possibly be involved. "He was for twenty years a most faithful slave," said the official report of the rebellion. "He maintained such an irreproachable character, and enjoyed so much the confidence of the whites, that when he was accused of leading the rebellion, not only was the charge discredited, but he was not even arrested for several days. . . . Not a symptom of the raging volcano within him had ever appeared. . . .''

The most common form of resistance was simply not to work very hard, or to be careless and do the job badly, or to break the equipment. An overseer in Mississippi named Carter, for example, nearly lost the cotton crop he was growing because the slaves only pretended to be working. When grass threatened to crowd out the young cotton, "all hands slighted their work by covering up the grass lightly, and not cutting it up . . . plows running about, and plowing a spot here, and a spot there, and where they did plow, they would let the plows run over the grass and not plow it up,'' someone reported.

Another traveler in the South stopped to watch an overseer working with slaves in South Carolina. He was "constantly directing and encouraging them,'' the traveler said, "but . . . as often as he visited one end of the line of operations, the hands at the other end would discontinue their labor, until he turned to ride toward them again.'' One Southern doctor thought that this unwillingness to work was so serious that it must be caused by a disease limited only to black people.

But slave resistance could take more serious forms, too. Arson was one. The newspapers and letters of the slaveowners are full of the fear of arson. A typical case occurred in 1844. Colonel William H. Taylor's plantation house, called Mount Airy, was destroyed by a fire set by a slave named Lizzy Flood. In the first five months of 1850, slaves were convicted of seven different cases of arson in Virginia alone. In Louisiana later that same year, seven different sugar factories were burned by slaves.

A CONTEST OF WILLS

Another slave weapon was poison. Slaves handled the food and did the cooking for many households in the South, and if they were inclined to revenge against their master, poison was always one possibility. Back in 1751, South Carolina had to enact a special law giving the death penalty to slaves who tried to poison whites. The reason given for the law was that the crime was so common. Ten years later a South Carolina paper said, alarmed, "The negroes have again begun the hellish practice of poisoning." Georgia offered a reward to informers who would help catch poisoners, because, "the detestable crime of poisoning hath frequently been committed by slaves." Five slaves were convicted of poisoning in Maryland in 1755. Two others were convicted in Virginia in 1803. Such convictions were not common, but they were far from rare. Almost any slaveowner could have told you stories of real or suspected murders by poison.

The masters constantly tried to control their slaves and impose their will upon them. The owners disagreed though on how this was best done. Some masters insisted that kindness and fair treatment were the only way to handle slaves effectively. Others were firmly convinced that harsh treatment and strong punishment were the way. Kindness, said this group, merely "spoiled" the slaves. They were sure slaves responded only to force.

The masters had plenty of force to use. The simplest and by far the commonest way to discipline slaves was to use the whip. Many owners or overseers carried a whip with them constantly because they might use it at any time. Sometimes slaves were hit with the whip on the

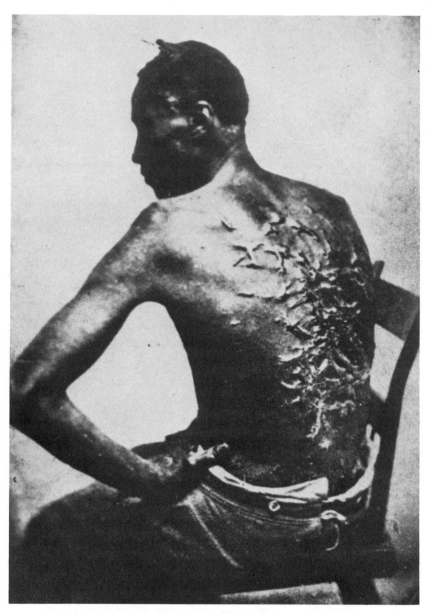

A lifetime of whippings left this slave's back a mass of scars. This photograph was taken by a Union army officer in the Civil War.

spur of the moment, at the time the master was angered. Sometimes it would be later, and the beating would be more organized, perhaps by tying the slave to a tree or post to administer the whipping. Men and women alike were whipped, usually across the bare back. Short or long whips, sticks, branches, leather belts, wooden paddles, it all added up to the same thing. The slaves lacked any reason to work for another man. They had no hopes and nothing to gain. In the contest of wills, the master had force, and only force, to get what he wanted.

Other punishments could be thought of, like extra work or the cancelling of some privilege. Sometimes an owner would combine reward and punishment. One master told his slaves that if they finished the harvest season on time and did good work, they could have a holiday and a barbecue. If they did not finish, however, they would all get half rations of food and a whipping. He reported that they finished, and got their barbecue. Some masters would sell their slaves away to the far South as punishment, never to see family and friends again. Being "sold South" was a grim threat, because the plantations down that way were large and impersonal, and had a reputation for working slaves mercilessly.

More than once or twice in the history of slavery in the United States a slave was killed by the master. But contrary to what might be expected, this was not always regarded as murder. If the death occurred in the process of "correcting" the slave, and if killing him were not the real purpose but only an accident, the slaveowner might well go unpunished. If the death took place on an isolated plantation, who would tell the authorities, and how would people know? A black person could not testify in court against a white. If there were no white witnesses, the killer could probably go free. There were cases where owners were brought to trial, convicted of killing their slave, and punished. How likely this was depended a lot on public opinion among the whites in the community. In older, settled regions the owners tended to police each other better; on the frontier the slave was in a more precarious position because the power of opinion was much weaker.

Back in colonial times, before the Revolution, it was not considered a serious crime to kill a slave. In many colonies, killing a slave was technically a misdemeanor, meaning a small crime, rather than a felony, or major one. By the 1800s though, the laws got a little tougher. In some exceptional cases, white people were convicted of murder for killing a slave. A North Carolina man beat his female slave with clubs, chains, and other weapons until she died. The court ordered this master hanged. In Kentucky two distant relatives of Thomas Jefferson's were found guilty of murdering a slave with an ax. In Mississippi some years later, a man was hanged for killing another man's slave. Many times, however, killing someone else's slave was not murder, but trespassing on the other's property. The only punishment was to pay the cash value of the dead slave.

Perhaps the greatest irony in the whole situation was that a slave's best protection as a human being was his value as property. Slaveowners used to complain that they were criticized unfairly for cruelty to their slaves, that such stories were exaggerated. After all, they said, these people are valuable, an investment, so why would we hurt, kill, or cripple them? But in a rough land, in a time when life was harsh and the law not very powerful, it would happen that slaves were hurt, crippled, or even killed.

Consider Frederick Douglass. He became a free man and the most powerful leader of blacks in America during the time of slavery. But as a young man he was a slave, and he endured and eventually won a classic contest of will with the slavemaster.

Raised in the city of Baltimore as a young boy, Douglass was not used to the rigors of farm slavery when, as a teenager, he was sold to Mr. Thomas Auld, on the Eastern Shore of Maryland. "He found me unsuitable," Frederick Douglass remembered later. "One of my greatest faults was that of letting his horse run away and go down to his father-in-law's farm. . . . I would then have to go after it. My reason for this kind of carelessness, or carefulness, was, that I could always get something to eat when I was there. Master William Hamilton, my master's father-in-law, always gave his slaves enough to eat. I never left there hungry."

Finally, Mr. Auld could tolerate it no more. He had given Douglass several whippings, none of which had done the slightest good. So he summoned Douglass and told him he was sending him to spend a year with a man named Edward Covey. The idea was simple; Covey had a reputation as a man who could break the spirit of the stubbornest slave.

It was January when Douglass went to Covey's farm. Within a week the city-bred black teenager had given

CAPTIVE BODIES, FREE SPIRITS

Covey cause for anger. Douglass had been unable to control a team of oxen on a trip into the woods for lumber. The day was largely wasted, and a fence gate had been broken. Covey was furious and ordered Douglass back to the woods. There the master cut three fresh switches from a tree and told the slave to take off his clothes. When Douglass did not move, the white man flew at him in a rage, ripped off his shirt, and beat him on the back until all three switches were worn out. It was, Douglass remembered, "a very severe whipping, cutting my back, causing the blood to run, and raising ridges on my flesh as large as my little finger." And this was only the first of the beatings Douglass would endure in the coming months as Edward Covey tried to make him meek and obedient.

Covey never let up in his vigilance over the slaves. He was both sly and cunning, and when he was not actually watching the slaves, they could still never be sure he would not be around somewhere. He once crawled on hands and knees through a tall stand of corn and then jumped up in the middle of the startled slaves, yelling at them and telling them to work faster. Another time he set out on what was supposed to be a five-hour trip to town and back, but only thirty minutes later Douglass saw him standing in a fence corner by the woods, watching.

On a hot August afternoon, Edward Covey finally pushed Frederick Douglass too far. While cleaning wheat and separating it from the chaff, Douglass collapsed in the heat. He could work no more. Covey came to where the boy lay and ordered him to get up. Douglass tried, but he fell. Covey took up a large hickory board and struck Douglass across the head. Douglass began to bleed from the wound, and he lay there unmoving despite Covey's kicks and curses. When Covey left him lying there, Douglass struggled to his feet, and headed for the woods. He was going to try to get back to Mr. Auld and out of this endless misery.

Covey spotted him, but Douglass made it to the woods and got out of sight. He collapsed in the woods again, and lay there for a long time. He feared he might bleed to death from the gash on his scalp, but the matted hair and dirt clotted the blood. After seven miles of thrashing through dense woods, he came to Auld's house, and, covered with scratches, blood, and mud, tried to tell his story. Auld's response was to tell Douglass he could spend the night to rest up, but must return to Covey the next day.

The next day was Saturday, and Douglass spent it again hiding in the woods. On Sunday, he finally decided to go back and face things. He had nowhere to go, nothing to eat. He was only sixteen. He went up the path to the house, and to his shock, Covey spoke kindly to him, and told him to drive some pigs out of a nearby field. Then Douglass understood. This was Sunday, and Covey, being a very religious man, was on his way to church. The crisis would not come until Monday.

Douglass was working in the barn when Covey came in on Monday. As the boy was coming down from the loft, Covey tried to wrap a rope around his feet, and began tying him up. Douglass tried to spring away and was thrown to the ground. But when Covey came upon him, something in Douglass snapped. Instead of taking his beating, he seized Covey by the throat and struggled to his feet. Covey began to shake, hanging on to Douglass even as the slave had him by the neck. Covey called to a slave named Hughes for help, and the other slave tried to tie Douglass's right hand. Douglass, never letting go of Covey, kicked Hughes hard below the ribs. Hughes doubled up and fell away. Really scared now, Covey tried to drag Douglass over to a large stick, but when he reached for the stick, Douglass threw him to the ground. For the next two hours they fought, the other slaves refusing to help either side. Finally, they both got to the point of sheer exhaustion, Covey bloody this time. Covey was helpless. Like the classic bully, he did not know what to do when someone fought back with heart and determination. His bluff was called.

Douglass remained with Covey for six more months, but never received another beating. The white man was afraid to risk it, afraid he might lose. Most of all, Douglass figured later, Covey didn't want anyone to know that this time the slave had won the contest of wills, and the slavebreaker had been broken.

From that time onward Douglass was determined to be free. He had felt his self-respect return, and he knew he could not endure slavery forever. It would be several years after the fight with Covey before Douglass made good his escape, but his determination was forged in that bloody battle in the farmyard.

Few slaves managed to assert themselves as strongly or as successfully as Frederick Douglass. Usually the struggle for supremacy went to the master, or at least the slave's resistance was less dramatic. Sometimes the refusal to be a slave expressed itself in tragic ways. Some individuals committed suicide rather than stay in bondage. Some tried to run, and met death rather than return.

Perhaps no slave's story is more painful than that of an unnamed man Frederika Bremer saw sitting dejected in a slave jail in Richmond, Virginia, in 1851, with a huge bandage on his right hand. She asked the jailer about him, and learned he was being held as a runaway until his master could come for him. The master had threatened to "sell him South," away from his wife and children, so the man had run away. Caught now, he was desperate to do something to keep from being sold. He had asked the jailer for an ax, to pound in some loose nails in his shoe. Suspecting nothing, the jailer gave it to him. "He is a very bad rascal," the jailer told Miss Bremer. "To be revenged upon his master, and to make himself fetch a less sum of money, (he) has cut off the fingers of his right hand!"

Such were the stakes in the steady battle between master and slave.

CHAPTER 7

Runaways and "Railroads"

THE HUNTER HAD stayed late in the swampy woods of Louisiana. Carrying a bag of five birds and his heavy gun, he began to find his way back to the farm where he was staying. His dog, Plato, kept pace with him, sometimes dashing a bit ahead, but mostly trotting at the hunter's side. He was as tired as his master. This hunter was not just an ordinary shooter looking for food, however. He was John James Audubon, one of the most famous naturalists in American history. It was the late 1820s. Audubon had taken the birds to stuff and paint them as part of his research into American wildlife. He had little idea of the adventure he was walking into.

Audubon reached a bayou, or slow, nearly still stream, which he was afraid was too deep to wade across. He threw his bag of birds across, then his rifle, powder flask, and bag of lead bullets. Then he and Plato began to wade, and for a few strokes, to swim, across the bayou. He kept his knife ready, because he was worried about alligators in those waters. He reached the other shore without incident, though, and was reaching over to pick up his gun when a deep voice said, "Stand still, or die!"

RUNAWAYS AND "RAILROADS"

Plato stiffened, bared his teeth, and began to growl. Audubon snatched the gun and came up with it cocked, looking for the man who had challenged him. In a moment, a tall black man stood up slowly from his hiding place in the woods and came forward, his rusty old gun aimed at Audubon's chest. The two men stood there for a second or two, each ready to shoot the other.

Audubon looked carefully at the man, and saw not so much a threat as a man really frightened. The black man's gun looked so ancient and beat up that it might not even work. Carefully, Audubon put his rifle down, tapped Plato to be quiet, and asked the stranger what he wanted. Instantly the man relaxed and lowered his gun, too.

"Master," he said with a mixture of dignity and fear, "I am a runaway. I might perhaps shoot you down; but God forbids it. . . . I ask mercy at your hands. For God's sake, do not kill me, master!"

Audubon asked him why he lived in the swamps instead of with his owner, but the slave did not want to tell his story just then. Instead, he offered to take Audubon to his camp in the swamps since it was too late for the naturalist to make it out of the woods before dark. In the morning, the slave said, he would guide Audubon to the main road, and even help him carry his birds.

Audubon, realizing the man was probably right about the time, agreed, but said he would follow behind the slave. Seeing that Audubon was still suspicious, the black man took the flint out of his old gun so it would not fire, and he gave that and his hunting knife to Audubon. Audubon told him to keep both, as they would need them if they met a bear or cougar. He had chosen to trust this sad, desperate man who was nonetheless ready to help a white man caught too late in the swamp.

With a perfect sense of direction, the slave led his guest on a difficult journey across bayous and through the heavy forest. He was very careful, and as he helped Aububon over fallen trees and through the tangled underbrush, Audubon could not help but notice that he was both strong and very familiar with the terrain. They entered a patch of grass higher than their heads. They sometimes had to crawl on hands and knees to get along.

Suddenly the slave gave out a loud cry, like the sound of an owl. Startled, Audubon levelled his gun at the man. "No harm, master," the slave said quickly, "I only give notice to my wife and children that I am coming." With that, he led Audubon into a clearing in the reeds.

They had made a regular camp, this runaway slave and his wife and their three children. Venison was roasting on a clean, smokeless fire. Sweet potatoes were cooking in the ashes. Before long the children were playing with Plato, Audubon had had a good meal, and the slave was cleaning Audubon's gun. The campfire was extinguished, and they made a small lantern by putting a burning pine knot in a hollowed-out gourd. By its light, the slave couple told the naturalist their heartbreaking story.

A year and a half earlier, the slave family had been put up for sale. Their master had had some severe financial losses, and he had to sell off his most valuable slaves. Since no one wanted to buy an entire family, they were auctioned off separately. The man was bought by the overseer from the same plantation because he was such a good worker. His wife was sold to a planter living nearly a hundred miles away. His three children went to plantations along the Mississippi River, even farther away. No one had meant to be deliberately unkind; the planter felt rather badly about the whole thing. But business was business, and slaves were property first and people second, and no law in Louisiana said that the slave family had to be respected.

The man was crushed with grief. For days after the sale, he was literally sick with anguish and would hardly move from his bed. His new owner began to think he had made a bad purchase. Then, in the middle of the night during a furious thunderstorm, the slave disappeared. From that day until he met Audubon, no white man had seen him.

His first stop had been the swamps, which he knew well, to build this camp in the tall cane. Then, one by one, he found his wife and then each of his children, and smuggled them away from their new owners by night. In time they were all reunited here in the wilds, living by their wits, and on what the father could catch or shoot. Slaves at their old plantation helped them by smuggling food out to them when they could.

Their success so far had been remarkable, but how long could they go on? How many weeks, months, years, could this brave family live out in the open, hiding by day and living by luck and stolen food? They knew their situation was desperate.

75

CAPTIVE BODIES, FREE SPIRITS

"Good master," the man pleaded with Audubon when he had finished his story, "for God's sake, do something for us and our children!"

Audubon stayed with them that night. The next morning he led them back to the planter who had sold them. The planter was very glad to see them. Touched by their story, he agreed to keep them. His finances having improved since he sold them, he paid their new owners for their value and kept them. Whether they remained secure as a family after that, Audubon did not know.

This story was remarkable and unusual, but runaways were not. Of all the ways slaves tried to fight back, running away was the most common. Literally tens of thousands of slaves ran away. Most of them were caught because the chances of being captured were great. And a captured runaway could be sure of drastic punishment. Yet year after year in the South, slaves left the only life they knew and made a desperate try for freedom, even if it was only the freedom of living like a hunted animal. The same doctor who invented a "disease" to account for slaves' laziness also invented one that seemed to account for the fact that they ran away so often.

Some slaves never got very far from home. Like the man in the swamp, they were hiding nearby, or as the old slave phrase called it, "laying out."

Charles and Peter were two slaves who ran away from their owner, Charles Sandiford, in 1845. Since they lived on a large island off the Georgia coast, it was hard to get completely away. They hid out in the woods and lived mostly by stealing and the help of their friends who were still on the plantation. Some planters out for a hunt saw them and chased them, but they got away into the marsh. The next day one of the planters heard that a sheep was missing, and he found it slaughtered and ready to be butchered for meat in the cabin of a slave named Sancho. Sancho claimed that Charles, the runaway, had put it there. Sancho said Charles, Peter, and some others were hiding in the woods nearby, but the planters could not find them. One of the owners was sure that Sancho was helping the runaways, and he was probably right.

That night Charles was spotted again, this time with a runaway named Dick. Both escaped again. The following night Charles and Dick were caught tying up a pair of sheep to steal them for food. Dick was captured, but

Capturing a runaway with dogs and guns: a nineteenth-century view.

CAPTIVE BODIES, FREE SPIRITS

Charles knocked down the man who came after him, and got away. After that, the planter's diary that gave us the story does not mention them again, and we do not know what became of them.

The family in the swamp, and Dick, Peter, and Charles were just a few of the many, many runaways who lived as fugitives, sometimes for years. In some of the larger swamps of the South there were groups of runaways, desperate communities living where everyone else was afraid to go.

For many runaways, however, "laying out" in the neighborhood was not the end of it. They wanted real freedom. They wanted to be away from slavery and the land that allowed it. They knew, somehow, that to the north was a place where slavery was not legal, a place where they might be free. They headed north.

James Pennington, a Maryland blacksmith, was a slave who dreamed of running away. He knew he was close to free territory in Pennsylvania, but he did not know how far it was, only that it was "north." He worried about what would happen to his father and mother, or to his ten brothers and sisters. Would they be punished or sold if he ran away? And he thought about what would happen to him if he failed.

"Yet of one thing there could be no mistake," he wrote years later, "that the consequences of a failure would be most serious. Within my recollection no one had attempted to escape from my master; but I had many cases in my mind's eye, of slaves of other planters who had failed, and who had been made examples of the most cruel treatment, by flogging and selling to the far South, where they were never to see their friends." In the end, though, "no consideration, not even that of life itself, could tempt me to give up the thought of flight."

Pennington's escape was typical. He hated to leave family and friends, but he was determined to have freedom. He traveled by night, hid by day. All he had to eat in three days was some bread and a few apples. He drank from streams. He found his way by looking for the North Star, the one star in the heavens that keeps its position constant throughout the seasons.

(The North Star guided many an escaping slave. When Frederick Douglass escaped and began a newspaper, he called it *The North Star,* because that was the guiding light to freedom. On cloudy nights, slaves would feel around trees for the moss, because moss usually grows only on the north side of trees.)

Still, Pennington got lost. He had traveled far enough to be in Pennsylvania, but he was on the Great National Road, only eighteen miles west of Baltimore. He was afraid to be on this road because traveling slaves were always challenged to see if they could prove their identity, and if they had freedom papers proving they were not slaves. Once a young white man asked Pennington if he were traveling far. James said yes. The youth asked him if he had papers. James said no.

"Well, my friend," said the kindly young man, "you should not travel on this road; you will be taken up before you have gone three miles. There are men living on this road who are constantly on the lookout for your people; and it is seldom that one escapes them who attempts to pass by day." Frightened, Pennington thanked him and hurried on, returning to the woods at his first chance.

He was caught later that same day. By playing ignorant, he bought some time. Then, while some men were taking him to see a judge to decide what to do with him, he tripped one of them and ran for it. The men chased him. He was nearly exhausted, and thinking of turning to fight his pursuers, when he ran over the top of a ridge right into a man plowing a field. Now he was caught for the second time.

Even later on that same day, unguarded for a moment, he made a second escape, leaped a fence, and managed to hide in the woods. A few nights and several miles later, he was in safe Pennsylvania, where some friendly white people helped him.

Eventually, James Pennington made his way to New York. He became a pastor in a Presbyterian church, and saved up enough money to pay his old master for his freedom. Not even slavery had destroyed this man's sense of honor.

One of the most ingenious runaway plans was that of Ellen and William Craft. Husband and wife, they nevertheless lived nearly one hundred miles apart because they were owned by different masters. William, a skilled mechanic, managed to arrange to get himself "hired out" by his master, and he saved up some money. The key part of the plan, however, was that Ellen did not look like a black person. She could fool strangers into thinking she was white.

In addition to the money they had saved, the Crafts stole some fancy clothes and headed, not north, but east, toward the seacoast. Since they were running away from Georgia, they knew it was too far to carry out their daring scheme over land. Instead, they would try to escape by sea. Ellen dressed up in man's clothing and pretended she was a white planter and that William was her personal slave. With this disguise they managed to travel by coach and stay at fine hotels, even in big cities like Charleston, South Carolina, where they caught a boat north to Philadelphia. The hardest part of their plan was that a "white man," as Ellen pretended to be, would have to register at hotels and sign a name, and neither of them could read or write. They solved that problem by bandaging Ellen's hand and claiming it was injured; the clerks signed the registers for her. The escape was successful.

Few slaves would have had the ingenuity, money, and opportunity the Crafts had. For most, especially in the deep South, there would be no escape without some help. Slaves along the way might give food and shelter, but not all of them could be trusted. There were rewards for turning in runaways. Some "bounty hunters" made a living tracking down fugitive slaves and sending them home. Owners put advertisements in the newspapers describing their runaways. Sometimes they would track slaves with dogs. A runaway needed help from people he could trust who knew what to do and where to go.

In America there were people who felt that slavery was wrong, and who were willing to help runaway slaves. These people, white and black alike, organized themselves to help slaves escape. This organization began as early as the Revolutionary War. At first most of the people in it were white members of a church called the

CAPTIVE BODIES, FREE SPIRITS

Society of Friends, or Quakers. Quakers thought slavery was a sin. They did not allow any of their members to own slaves. Some Quakers even broke the law and helped slaves get away to freedom.

Later, by the 1830s, hundreds of people felt that way, and not only Quakers. Their organization was never very formal. They never had any national meetings. They barely had a name. But when one slaveowner chasing a runaway lost track of him near the Ohio River, he complained that it was as if the slave had disappeared on an "underground road."

The phrase stuck, and the slave-escape network became known as "the Underground Railroad." The houses on the way to freedom were called "stations." The people who guided the runaways were "conductors." Their work was illegal and often dangerous, but without it most slaves would never have made it to freedom.

The "railroad" ran at night. In the beginning the runaways were mostly men, mostly traveling on foot. After 1830 the traffic increased. Large groups of slaves were smuggled out of the South—men, women, and children. The "conductors" used covered wagons, farm wagons, whatever was big enough. Some people had special compartments built into the bottom of their wagons for hiding runaways.

The "stations" were close together, usually ten or twenty miles apart, because it was not easy to travel far at night. Slaves hid in attics, barns, cellars, even secret rooms. The "railroad" began anywhere in the South the slaves could find it, and ran deep into the North. Ohio

RUNAWAYS AND "RAILROADS"

was the busiest route west of the Appalachian Mountains. Pennsylvania and New Jersey were active in the East.

But why was the railroad in the North? Weren't runaway slaves safe once they reached "free" soil where slavery was not legal?

No, they were not safe. Legally, they were still someone's property. By law, they were supposed to be returned to their owner. If they were caught by the owner or his agents, even in the North, they would be taken to court and ordered returned. Many Northerners did not like black people any better than the Southerners did, and did not at all mind turning in a fugitive slave for the reward. The professional bounty hunters were always on the lookout for runaways in the North.

By one estimate, over 3,200 people worked actively in the Underground Railroad. They not only gave their time, they raised money—money for food, train tickets, clothes, and supplies. Some of their stories are remarkable.

Calvin Fairbanks was a college-educated white man who began to travel the South in 1837 to help slaves escape. He would guide them through Kentucky and across the Ohio River into the free state of Ohio. One of his accomplices was a schoolteacher we know only as Miss Webster. Runaways would pose as her servants, and she would help them escape that way. None of Fairbanks's fugitives was ever captured, but he spent many years in jail for what he was doing. It didn't stop him.

John Fairfield was white. He was also a Southerner and his family owned slaves. Yet he grew up hating slavery, and when he left the South, he took a slave

Runaways in the rain: slave families fleeing to the
North, nineteenth century.

friend with him. Since this slave was someone else's
property, the white people of Fairfield's hometown in
Virginia tried to have him arrested for slave stealing.
Other runaways in the North heard of what he had done,
and they asked for his help. He could not refuse. So
began an amazing career of going to the South to find
and bring out particular individual slaves whose families
were waiting for them in the North.

Fairfield was a wonderful actor. He played the part of a
slave owning planter, a poultry and egg peddler, even a
slave trader. He made trips into most states of the deep
South. He was always broke, or almost so, and suffered
many hardships. Once he was shot. But he never quit,
and he delivered many slaves to Canada, or to his
Quaker friend in Ohio, Levi Coffin. (Coffin helped so
many slaves escape—perhaps as many as three thousand

RUNAWAYS AND "RAILROADS"

—that he was often referred to as the "President" of the Underground Railroad.) Once, Fairfield delivered twenty-eight runaways at once by organizing them into a pretended "funeral procession."

Many black people, most of them former slaves themselves, worked on the Underground Railroad. Josiah Henson, whose story of being sold away from his mother was told earlier, was one. Another was Elijah Anderson. Anderson led more than 1,000 slaves to freedom from 1850 to 1855, and then he was captured himself. He died in a Kentucky prison in 1857. John Mason was a fugitive slave from Kentucky, but he took the risks of returning to lead out others. He once led a total of 265 people to Canada in a year and a half. On one of his missions he was captured and resold into slavery, but he escaped again. Before he was finished, he had guided 1,300 runaways.

The greatest conductor of them all was Harriet Tubman. She was a frail woman, not very healthy, and she could not read or write. Yet after she escaped herself, she made nineteen dangerous trips into the South to bring out others. Her own sister, mother, and father were among the hundreds of slaves she conducted to freedom. Like Fairfield, she was a great natural actor, clever at playing the role of a dumb slave woman who could not possibly be any threat. In fact, she was brave and shrewd. She usually began her escapes on Saturday night, because it was harder for the masters to get organized and advertise for their runaways on Sunday. She kept an iron discipline over the runaways who traveled with her, threatening to kill any who turned back, because they would jeopardize the others. Harriet Tubman was never caught.

How many slaves escaped? It is impossible to tell exactly. There are no good records. But we know that advertisements for runaways were an everyday thing in Southern newspapers. We know that Southern planters were very angry about the runaway problem and the Underground Railroad. One historian who has looked into the question carefully, believes that in the forty years between 1810 and 1850 over one hundred thousand slaves made the perilous journey into freedom.

CHAPTER 8

Revolt!

THE OTHER SLAVES could scarcely believe it. Nat Turner had come back. He had run away, just as his father had many years before. Most of the slaves on the Virginia plantation figured that he had made it to the North. He had been gone so long the master had stopped looking for him. Actually, Nat Turner had just been hiding out in the woods.

He came back because he had other plans. He said later that he had a vision while he was hiding in the woods, and in that vision voices told him that it was selfish for him to run away. Nat Turner believed that he was destined to lash out against slavery in a far greater way than just running away. So he came back to accept his punishment and to wait for the day when his vision would be painted in blood.

The other slaves always found Nat to be strange, unpredictable, and maybe a little scary. He was undoubtedly intelligent, possibly gifted. Born around the year 1801, he grew up in Southampton, Virginia. He virtually taught himself to read and write as a small child. He was intensely religious, and became something of a preacher for the other slaves. By the time he returned from his escape to the woods, the other slaves thought of him as a mystic, a man in touch with the spirits, a man who had visions. They would follow where Nat Turner would lead them.

When odd things happen in nature, people sometimes take it as a sign, a signal that a special time is at hand. When there was an eclipse of the sun in February, 1831, Nat Turner saw it as his cue to follow his destiny. That destiny, he said later, was shown to him in several dreams. "I saw white spirits and black spirits engaged in battle," he reported, "and the sun was darkened—the thunder rolled in the heavens, and blood flowed in streams."

Later that year, Nat followed his dream. He gathered some friends in the woods late in the day on Sunday, August 21, 1831. Henry, Hark, Sam, Nelson, Will, and Jack met Nat with some food and brandy and made their desperate plan. What stands out most of all in the tragic story of Nat Turner's slave revolt is the desperation of these men.

Two hours after dark on that Sunday night, it began. The men went to the home of the planter, named Travis, who owned Nat. Hark got a ladder, and Nat climbed to a second-story window, entered, and crept downstairs to open the door for the others. They first took the guns they found in the house, then went upstairs carrying their other weapons of axes and knives as well. Led by the mysterious Nat and angered by a lifetime of slavery, they killed the entire family of five—even the infant baby.

Throughout a night of revenge and horror, Nat Turner and his growing band swept across the farmland of

REVOLT!

Southampton County, killing white families and adding more slaves to their small army. They acquired horses, and more guns, more men. They killed every white person they met, without exception, and moved quickly. Their first target was to be the small town of Jerusalem, Virginia, where they could gather more supplies. What their ultimate goal was isn't known. They were in open, bloody revolt throughout Sunday night and Monday morning.

When they reached the Porter farm, the slaves found that the family had fled. That meant that the alarm had been given, and that the whites now knew what was happening. It still took some time for the whites to get organized to stop the growing slave revolt. It was late Monday before white troops were looking for Turner's men.

Led only by Turner's fierce determination, the slaves were not well organized or armed, nor very experienced in fighting. Once the militia attacked them, they could not hold. Slaves fled in all directions. Many were killed immediately. Most of those who were arrested were quickly hanged, fifty-five of them.

Across this out-of-the-way section of rural southeastern Virginia, nearly sixty white people lay dead, victims of Turner's revolt. And Nat Turner himself was still at large.

For weeks Turner hid out in a small hole he dug under a pile of fence rails in the woods. He had some supplies from the Travis farm. He came out of hiding for only a few minutes each night to get water from a stream. He was discovered accidentally by a hunting dog who smelled some of the meat in Turner's hideout. He fled from that place to another tiny hole he had scratched out under a fallen tree. It was there that he was discovered by a white man named Phipps. Phipps leveled his pistol at Turner, and the fiery slave surrendered quietly, probably exhausted, and now willing to accept the rest of what fate had in store for him. His only remaining weapon was a sword. After two weeks in jail, heavily guarded and bound in chains, Nat Turner was hanged on November 11, 1831.

Nat Turner's terrible revolt was the bloodiest the plantation system of the South ever knew, but it was far

The capture of Nat Turner.

from the only one. Indeed, one of the first big slave uprisings in the English colonies of North America was not even in the South at all, but in New York City in 1712, when slavery was still legal there. Nine whites were killed in that revolt, and later twenty-seven blacks died, twenty-one by execution and six by suicide. These six preferred to die by their own hand rather than be captured.

This early slave uprising set the pattern. The white masters were caught by surprise, but as soon as they could recover from the shock and bring out the army, the blacks were overpowered. In some cases, the revolt was betrayed before it began by a slave who was let in on the plot. Sometimes the slaves were just trying to get away. Sometimes it appeared there wasn't a clear goal, just anger and revenge.

The slaves of Stono, South Carolina, were trying to escape overland to Spanish territory in Florida when they rebelled in 1739. They began on a Sunday, as Nat Turner would do in 1831, and marched across the country toward St. Augustine, Florida. They did not kill everyone in their path. A tavernkeeper named Wallace was spared because he was a kind man and good to his slaves. Another slaveowner, Mr. Rose, was saved by his own slaves, who hid him and talked the rebels into going away without doing any harm. Yet, at other places, the rebels killed all the whites they saw, including the children. They had a flag of some sort, and two drums to march by. In the end, white South Carolina soldiers intercepted them, killing many, and capturing the rest.

One of the biggest slave plots came close to success,

but slaves who knew of it told the whites. The leader was named Gabriel, sometimes called Gabriel Prosser because his master's name was Prosser. The plot involved at least a thousand slaves, and as many as five thousand knew of it. On August 30, 1800, slaves by the hundreds met at a point six miles from the city of Richmond, Virginia. They had been preparing for months, making plans and gathering weapons. The authorities were warned by two slaves, but the plot might still have succeeded except for a violent afternoon thunderstorm that stopped the marching slaves and washed out an important bridge on the road to the city. Given the extra time, the militia counterattacked, defeated the slave army, and arrested the leaders. Thirty-five slaves were executed, including Gabriel himself, who refused to talk to the authorities even though he was on trial for his life.

One of the Gabriel Plot slaves did talk, however, and his words must have stung the white Virginians who were proud of their role in the American Revolution. "I have nothing more to offer," said the captured slave, "than what General Washington would have had to offer, had he been taken by the British. . . . I have ventured my life in endeavouring to obtain the liberty of my countrymen, and am a willing sacrifice to their cause. . . ."

Sometimes free blacks who lived in the South were involved in plots to help slaves escape. One of the most famous was led by Denmark Vesey, in Charleston, South Carolina, in July 1822. Vesey had bought his own freedom in 1800 and was making a comfortable living as a carpenter in Charleston. He had no personal reason for rebelling against slavery. But he did. In fact, Vesey was so well off, so respected, and so highly thought of by the whites that many people had a hard time believing that he was behind it all. But he was.

Vesey, too, was betrayed by a slave who told his master of the plot. Knowing he had been turned in, Vesey tried to move up the date of the revolt by a month, but he could not get the word to his comrades scattered throughout the Charleston area. Over a hundred blacks, slave and free, were arrested. Thirty-five were executed, including Vesey. Even four white men were put in prison for helping in the plot. Had it been successful, thousands of slaves would have been involved.

There were many, many small revolts and plots of revolts by slaves in the South. It was one thing the whites were constantly afraid of. Slave revolts were not only frightening in their destruction and killing, they showed how desperate the slaves were.

The white owners always reacted by cracking down for a while on the slaves. The patrols became more active. Owners watched their slaves more carefully, and were more suspicious. After the Turner rebellion in 1831, many Southern states made it illegal to teach a slave to read and write. Such laws were common in the South, even before Turner, but after 1831 there was a new determination to enforce them. Reading and writing were dangerous. Slaves who could read and write could make plots and communicate with each other, or read literature put out by the Underground Railroad and other groups that hated slavery.

In some states it was even illegal for slaves to have horns, bells or drums, because in Africa people could communicate with each other using such instruments. The slaveowners were afraid the Africans who lived in slavery in America still remembered how to pass on a message on the drum.

Slave revolts made it harder, too, on the few free blacks who lived in the South. These people had become free in a variety of ways: by the will of their master, by buying their own freedom with wages they made doing extra work, or just because the master grew to feel it was wrong or inconvenient to own a slave. Once free, free blacks had free children. But the whites worried about having free black people around where the slaves could see them and know that it was possible to be both black and free. The free blacks did not lead a very good life, and most were poor, but at least they were their own masters. After the Denmark Vesey plot, whites became suspicious that the free blacks were plotting with the slaves.

The South reacted to the slave revolts with violence. The way to keep the peace, they felt, was to crack down hard. Wasn't Vesey a comfortable free man with a good trade as a carpenter? Wasn't Nat Turner a well-treated slave, a religious man who had learned how to read? If these men could turn on you, who was safe? So the whites tried to maintain control with force and fear.

Following a small slave uprising in Louisiana, the heads of sixteen rebels were put up on poles by the banks of the Mississippi River as a grim reminder of the fate that awaited those who rebelled—and failed.

CHAPTER 9

Fighting for Freedom: Part I

THE LETTER ARRIVED in the New York offices of a newspaper called *The Colored American* late in November, 1839. Inside the envelope was five dollars. The money was sent to help this weekly paper for black Americans, a paper founded by Samuel Cornish. The money had come from a group of black children in Pittsburgh, Pennsylvania, who had founded a "Juvenile Anti-Slavery Society." Since July, the forty young members of the society had paid dues of a penny a week. Their first contribution was to help the newspaper.

That children would save their pennies to support a newspaper meant something. It was not just the newspaper they believed in, it was the movement behind it. Black people in America had banded together to fight slavery and to bring it to an end.

Slaves could fight for their own personal freedom and strike back against their masters. But those outside slavery, the free blacks of the South and the North, could fight against slavery itself. They united in a crusade to get rid of slavery once and for all. They held meetings, wrote newspapers, and tried to get the laws changed. Most of all they tried to open the minds of the white people who controlled the nation and its laws.

Blacks and whites worked together to attack slavery. People who opposed slavery were called "antislavery." The most serious of the antislavery believers were called "abolitionists," because they wanted not just to limit slavery, or to criticize it, but to abolish it immediately, to get rid of it at once.

Criticism of slavery was an old issue in America. Serious antislavery groups had been started as early as the American Revolution, in the 1770s. By 1830 there were many antislavery organizations, and over fifty of them were made up primarily of black people. But around the year 1830 the antislavery movement began to change. It became more abolitionist, more radical. One of the people who contributed to this was David Walker.

David Walker had never been a slave himself. He was born of a free black mother in North Carolina. As an adult he lived in Boston, where he made a living as a dealer in secondhand clothes. But neither being free nor living in the North kept him from hating slavery. The pamphlet he wrote in 1829 had a long title, but it is commonly known as "David Walker's Appeal." Two things about it are important. First, it was an angry, passionate piece of writing. Walker thought that slavery was a terrible crime, and that it should be brought down by any means possible, even violence. Second, he was not just another white man criticizing his fellow white men; he was a black man speaking out angrily on the side of his suffering brothers. This was a surprise to people in 1829.

Walker caused quite a shock. In one Southern state where his pamphlet appeared people were so upset that they charged Walker with committing the crime of trying to start a slave revolt. They wanted the governor of Massachusetts to deport Walker to the South where they could put him on trial. The governor refused.

Two years after Walker's "Appeal," a weekly newspaper devoted to the abolitionist cause appeared. The editor was one of the white abolitionists the blacks most respected, William Lloyd Garrison. His newspaper was called the *Liberator*, and of his first 450 subscribers, 400 were black people.

Garrison had thought about slavery for a long time. He had worked with others, especially a Quaker named Benjamin Lundy, to put out antislavery newspapers. He had even spent time in jail for his activities. By 1831 he knew what he believed, and he was ready to speak his mind without holding back. When some people urged him to be quieter, more moderate, he said: "Moderation? Ask a mother whose baby has fallen into the fire 'moderately' to extract the infant from the flames, but do not ask me to be moderate on the question of slavery!"

Garrison's strong language and sense of his own rightness cost him a lot of friends and support. But black people generally approved of him because they, too, felt that strong words and hard actions would be necessary to bring down slavery. Living in the North after his escape from slavery, Frederick Douglass discovered the *Libera-*

SLAVE-BRANDING.

Abolitionists emphasized the cruel side of slavery, as in this drawing, from a nineteenth-century antislavery pamphlet, of slaves being branded for identification.

tor and loved it. It "took a place in my heart second only to the Bible," he said. Reading Garrison's words, and then hearing him speak, Douglass was in awe of the man. "He seemed to me an all-sufficient match to every opponent. . . . His words were full of holy fire, and straight to the point."

Many of the leaders of the antislavery movement were white—people like James G. Birney, who used to be a slaveholder, and Theodore Dwight Weld, who put together a book about the cruelty of slavery by using the Southerners' own words, letters, and newspaper stories. Some of the leaders were women, like Sarah and

FIGHTING FOR FREEDOM: PART I

Angelina Grimké, two sisters from South Carolina who had to leave the South because of their opposition to slavery.

One of the most important antislavery writings was not a newspaper or a pamphlet, but a novel. *Uncle Tom's Cabin* was published in the early 1850s by a white woman, Harriet Beecher Stowe. Though living in Maine by then, Mrs. Stowe had been active in antislavery work in Cincinnati for years. The slave stories she knew from that experience went into her novel. She was very kind to Southerners in the story; the nasty villain who beats old Uncle Tom to death, Simon Legree, was a Yankee from Vermont. What she was trying to say in this very emotional book was that the system of slavery itself was evil, however kind individual slaveowners might be. But the Southerners did not care about the message. They were just angry that this antislavery story became one of the fastest-selling books in all of American history, and that it made people think about the evil of slavery more than any number of newspaper stories or speeches could ever do.

On the other hand, a lot of white people in the North did not like the antislavery crusaders. It is clear that of all the white Northerners, at first only a few were really dedicated to ending slavery. The reason for this was simple: most white people in the North shared the Southerners' view of black people as inferior and unequal; prejudice was not limited to the land of slavery. And even those white people who were not prejudiced simply did not care what was going on a thousand miles away in the South. It was not their problem.

CAPTIVE BODIES, FREE SPIRITS

A big part of the antislavery program was to convince the majority of white Northerners that it *was* their problem. Abolitionists tried to show people that slavery was evil, that it violated the teachings of the Bible, and that it was bad for the country. But it was hard to get people to care about a problem they could not see.

Unlike the whites, the black community cared very much about slavery, because it was something that touched their lives deeply. Almost every free black person in the North had an ancestor who had been a slave. Every free black person in the North knew what it was like to face discrimination. The most outspoken of all were the runaway slaves, who were, in the words of one white abolitionist, graduates of the school of slavery "with their diploma written upon their back"—in scars.

When Frederick Douglass finally made his escape several years after his fight with the slavebreaker, Covey, he got help from some sympathetic white people to go north to New Bedford, Massachusetts. All he wanted to do was work hard as a free man and never again have to worry about slavery, or being sent back to Maryland. Instead, he became the greatest of the black abolitionists.

Douglass was so glad to be free when he got to Massachusetts in the year 1838 that even the prejudice he ran into did not make him sad. He had learned a skill as a young teenager living in Baltimore before he was sent down to the plantation to be a field laborer. He knew how to caulk wooden ships, sealing them against the water. But he was not allowed to take that job in New Bedford because the white workers would not work with a black man. They would all have quit if Douglass had been hired. Therefore, instead of earning two dollars a day at a skilled trade, Douglass earned one dollar a day as a common laborer. He sawed wood, shoveled coal, dug cellars, moved trash, loaded and unloaded ships, and cleaned ships' cabins.

In time he found regular work, first at an oil refinery (making oil for lamps, most likely) and then at a brass foundry. At the brassworks his job was to pump the bellows, which was a large device for blowing air into the fire to keep it hot. Douglass would spend long hours straining up and down on the huge beam handle of the bellows, keeping the flames fierce enough to melt metal.

Douglass worked hard and had little energy left for anything else. But he was a serious man, and happy to be able to run his own life and keep the simple wages he earned. He found time for reading by nailing copies of newspapers to the post near his bellows. As he pumped he would read, the sweat pouring off his face from the heat of the furnace. One of the newspapers given to him by a friend was a copy of the *Liberator*.

Reading Garrison's newspaper confirmed what Douglass already knew about slavery. More than that, it showed him that other people, some of them white, felt the same way he did. Garrison came to New Bedford to lecture on antislavery, and the young Douglass was in the audience, more impressed than ever. Still, three years after he had run away, Douglass did not think of himself as a crusader against slavery. All he knew was that he hated what had been done to him and was still being done to others. The only antislavery work he did was to talk to the sympathetic white workers about his life, and to lecture to his black friends at the church he attended every Sunday.

Then, in 1841, he finally took a few days off from work. His idea of a holiday was to go by boat over to the island of Nantucket where they were having a big antislavery meeting. To Douglass's surprise, one of the white organizers of the meeting had heard Douglass speak at the black church. This man asked Douglass at the last minute to speak to the convention.

Douglass was nearly frozen with fear at the thought of speaking before that crowd of a thousand people. "It was with the utmost difficulty that I could stand erect, or that I could command and articulate two words without hesitation and stammering. I trembled in every limb. I am not sure that my embarrassment was not the most effective part of my speech, if speech it could be called." The audience took to heart this nervous young black man and his touching true story of life as a slave. When William Lloyd Garrison himself took the stage immediately after Douglass, Garrison used Douglass's story as the basis for his own speech.

After the speeches, John Collins, head of the Massachusetts Anti-Slavery Society, came up to Douglass and offered him a job working for the Society. Douglass would travel through Massachusetts and nearby states, and help organize people to fight slavery by telling his own story. The Society would pay him to do this.

Douglass hesitated. He had a steady job and was just beginning to get ahead in life. He had been free for only three years. Besides, if he attracted too much attention, his master from Maryland might find out about him and try to recapture him, or have the courts send him back into slavery. But Collins insisted, and Douglass could not pass up a chance to work against slavery. He agreed to go on the road for the Massachusetts Anti-Slavery Society. He agreed to do this for three months only; after that he would go back to working in New Bedford.

Frederick Douglass never went back to his old job. As long as slavery existed in the United States, his career was to fight against it. It was a hard, lonely, often dangerous job.

The first problem he faced was the one he had feared. His growing fame made it possible for his old master to find him and come after him. Under the laws of Maryland, Frederick Douglass was still a piece of property. Even worse, as he became a better speaker, he made people wonder if he was telling the truth. How could such a smart, eloquent man ever have been a slave?

If he wanted to fight slavery by lecturing and organizing, Frederick Douglass knew he must risk recapture by telling the whole story of his life—names, dates, places. People had to be told so they would believe. Douglass wrote it all down, and prepared to publish it. His white abolitionist friend, Wendell Phillips, saw the danger. "Throw it into the fire!" he told Douglass when he had seen the manuscript. But Douglass went ahead with his plan. His hope was that if his owner tried to reclaim him, friends would pay the owner for Douglass's value. As it turned out, Douglass had become so famous that his old owner did not even try to get him back.

CAPTIVE BODIES, FREE SPIRITS

Recapture was not the only danger the black abolitionists faced. All abolitionists were unpopular in many towns. Some people blamed the abolitionists for causing Nat Turner's bloody revolt. They were regarded as noisy troublemakers. Abolitionists caused friction and arguments between North and South. They criticized the North, too, saying that it was the North's responsibility to help get rid of slavery and to treat free black people better. Many people did not like speakers coming into their town to tell them things they did not want to hear.

Mobs broke up antislavery meetings and threatened the speakers. White abolitionist Lewis Tappan had his house burned in New York. Theodore Weld was stoned and hit with rotten eggs in Ohio. Elijah Lovejoy in Illinois had three of his printing presses burned by mobs. When he and his friends tried to defend another one, he was shot and his body dumped into the Mississippi River. Even women were attacked. A meeting of the Massachusetts Female Anti-Slavery Society in Boston was broken up by a mob. The police had to lead the women to safety. They were almost too late to save William Lloyd Garrison from that same mob. He was beaten, and his clothes were torn. He was being dragged through the streets by a rope when the police arrested him for his own good and took him to jail for protection.

Most of the time Douglass worked in small towns in the Northeast, and his greatest problem was not mob threats but boredom and small crowds in tiny, out-of-the way places. He was on the road constantly. He stayed with sympathetic supporters where he could find them. He

Frederick Douglass in old age.

lectured in schoolhouses and churches, or on street corners and in parks if he had to. In the year 1843 he made over one hundred speeches in different towns.

But as a black man, Douglass was in even greater danger than the whites. The trouble began to mount as he worked his way west, through western New York state and into Ohio and Indiana. These last two states had many Southerners living in them, and the slave state of Kentucky was right next door. At Richmond, Indiana, Douglass's clothes were ruined by rotten eggs. At Pendleton they could not get anyone to let them use a building, so the local antislavery supporters built an outdoor platform. Just as Douglass was ready to speak to quite a large crowd, a mob of sixty "of the roughest characters I ever looked upon," Douglass remembered, rode up and ordered the meeting to break up. Douglass tried to talk to them, to get them to back off and listen. But these men did not come to talk. They came to fight.

They attacked. The platform was ripped apart and thrown to the ground. One of the organizers was hit in the mouth and lost several teeth. Another was smashed across the head with a club and cut badly. Douglass grabbed a stick and tried to fight his way clear, but the mob got him. Dozens of blows drove him to the ground. He was kicked repeatedly. When the fighting stopped and the thugs got back on their horses and rode away, Frederick Douglass lay unconscious, his right hand broken so badly that it was slightly deformed for the rest of his life.

Not even this stopped him, however, nor did it stop the other abolitionists, black and white, who were fighting for the end of slavery. Douglass went on to start his own abolitionist newspaper in 1845. He called it the *North Star,* after the runaway slaves' beacon to freedom.

Slowly, as the years passed, the fight of the runaway slaves and their white friends gained ground. Slavery was criticized more and more. A political party was organized to stop slavery, called the Liberty Party. When it failed, another one took its place, the Free Soil Party.

In 1850, the Southern states managed to get the Congress to pass the Fugitive Slave Law, which made it a federal crime to help or conceal a runaway slave. Instead of making slavery stronger, it made a lot of people in the North angry. They might not care if slavery were far away in the South, but they did not want to be involved in it by having to return runaway slaves. The great writer and philosopher, Ralph Waldo Emerson, was so angered by the fundamental inhumanity of the Fugitive Slave Law that he declared, "I will not obey it, by God!"

Anthony Burns was one of the runaways caught by the Fugitive Slave Law. He had been in Massachusetts for two months when he was picked up by the authorities. He was put in irons in the courthouse, and awaited trial to see whether he should be sent back to the South. Two top lawyers took on his case, Richard Henry Dana, a white man, and Robert Morris, who was black. They could get only a three-day delay in the trial. On the second day of Burns's captivity a small group of abolitionists tried to break into the jail to free him, but they failed.

Wendell Phillips, William Lloyd Garrison, and Theodore Parker gave speeches at a huge protest meeting in

Boston. The city was badly divided on the slavery issue. Many people sincerely wanted Burns to be free, and they resented that their own police and militia were being used to hold him captive. As the tension grew, soldiers took over the courthouse to prevent any other attempts at freeing Burns. Their guns poked from every window of the building.

On June 2, 1854, a week after the failed rescue attempt, Burns was found to be the rightful property of a Southern owner. The antislavery men were so angry that the authorities had to escort Burns, in irons, through the streets of Boston surrounded by soldiers. They marched him to the ship with bayonets fixed on the ends of their muskets. There was even a cannon ready to fire if the angry antislavery crowd should attempt to rescue him. He went back into slavery. We do not know what became of Anthony Burns.

In 1854, the tension between North and South over slavery grew even worse. There had been a law on the books which said that as America settled the West, no slavery would be allowed to the north side of a line drawn across the map. (This law was part of the Missouri Compromise, passed in 1820. On a map you can find the line limiting slavery by finding the long southern border of Missouri and extending it westward.) But in 1854 that line was erased, and it was decided to let the people who moved into the territories of the Great Plains choose for themselves whether to allow slavery.

This law of 1854, called the Kansas-Nebraska Act, made everything worse. It caused terrific fighting in that territory between those who wanted slavery and those who did not. It made many people in the North feel that slavery was no longer something far away that did not concern them. Now slavery was creeping out of the South, taking over the West, and threatening to surround the free states of the Northeast with a ring of slave states. One angry group of Northerners formed a new political party just to stop this spread of slavery. It was called the Republican Party. One of the men who joined it soon after it began was Abraham Lincoln.

By this time, in the middle 1850s, some runaway slaves and free blacks had just about given up on the United States as a place to live. Some of these people had gone to Canada, where there was no slavery at all and where there was less discrimination against black people. Others wanted to go farther—all the way back to Africa. Still others felt that Africa was too far away, and they looked instead for places in South America to go to.

As early as 1817, in fact, a group was formed to send blacks in the United States back to Africa. This group, called the American Colonization Society, was started and run by whites. They were alarmed by the growth of slavery in the United States, and they thought it might solve the problem if all black people could be sent back to Africa. After all, weren't they kidnapped from Africa in the first place?

But black Americans did not like the American Colonization Society and its program. A few days after the Society was started in Philadelphia, a huge meeting at a black church there unanimously agreed that the whole scheme was just a way to avoid giving black Americans their rights. In fact, a lot of slaveholders supported the American Colonization Society, not because they did not like slavery but because they wanted to get rid of the *free* blacks in the South, and thereby make slavery stronger.

The American Colonization Society did start a colony on the west coast of Africa in 1823. They called it Liberia, and it exists to this day. Its capital is named Monrovia, after James Monroe, who was president of the United States when Liberia came into existence.

Liberia never made a dent in slavery in the United States. Only a few desperate people wanted to go, and the cost of sending them was high. There were more slaves smuggled illegally into the United States *every few years* than were sent to Liberia in half a century. The Colonization Society eventually settled fifteen thousand slaves and former slaves in Liberia. By the late 1850s, however, there were four *million* slaves in the United States, and another half a million free blacks living in both the North and the South.

If the fight against slavery were to be won, it would not be by colonization. It would take a struggle, as abolitionists like Garrison and Weld and Douglass had been saying all along. But for them struggle meant hard work, the education of the American people, and changing the laws. For a man named John Brown, struggle meant something more direct, something violent.

John Brown was a white man who had spent fifty-five years of his life drifting through a series of jobs and

John Brown, who led the attempted slave rebellion at
Harper's Ferry, 1859.

businesses without any success. Until 1856 the most notable thing about him was that he was father to twenty children. Then he got caught up in the border wars in Kansas between the slavery and antislavery forces, and his life changed. Brown became a committed antislavery fighter, the leader of a band that killed several people. Eventually he had to flee Kansas as a wanted man. But his career as a guerrilla soldier against slavery and the South was far from over.

Brown wanted to strike a death blow to slavery. He convinced several rich and important antislavery men of the Northeast—a group called the Secret Six— to finance his dangerous plan.

What John Brown planned to do was to take a small band of black and white volunteers and attack the federal arsenal at Harper's Ferry, Virginia, where the army kept guns and ammunition. (Harper's Ferry is in West Virginia now.) Then they would issue a call for slaves to run away and join them, and give the slaves the guns. The next step would be to advance South through the Appalachian Mountains, gathering more and more runaways as they went, until John Brown's slave army would be too powerful to stop. All slaves would come to them, and slavery would be finished. Brown apparently thought of starting up his own country in the South; he had even written a constitution for this new country.

Late in September 1859, Frederick Douglass was at his home in Rochester, New York, when he received a message from John Brown. Douglass and Brown had been friends for more than ten years, and Brown had often talked about going into the South on a raid. Now he asked Douglass to meet him at a stone quarry outside of Chambersburg, Pennsylvania. Brown also wanted Douglass to bring whatever money he could and another runaway slave named Shields Green. Douglass went, and brought Green.

Douglass found John Brown disguised as a fisherman, living secretly in the quarry. Brown told Douglass he had changed his plan, and when Douglass heard about the planned attack on a federal arsenal, he feared the worst. He tried to tell Brown that it was foolish, even suicidal. But Brown would not be moved from his scheme. After two days, Douglass went away, fearful for his friend. Shields Green, however, remained with Brown.

It *was* a suicide mission. From the farmhouse on the Maryland side of the Potomac River where Brown and his men had their base, eighteen men moved out on Sunday night, October 16, 1859. Five were black, including Shields Green; the rest were white, and included a couple of Brown's own sons. They crossed the river on the railroad bridge in the dead of night, and captured the little town and the arsenal. But, as Douglass predicted, Brown's plan had no chance.

Brown had cut himself off from his base of supplies. He was in a town surrounded by mountains and two rivers and he had no real avenue of escape. There were not many slaves in this part of Virginia to come to his aid. When the army counterattacked, Brown's band holed up in the railroad engine house. A small company of United States Marines, led by a colonel named Robert E. Lee, stormed their position. It was all over as quickly as it began.

Brown's raid cost the life of one U.S. Marine and four of the people who lived in Harper's Ferry, including the mayor and a free black citizen of the town. Ten of Brown's men were killed, including two of Brown's sons. Five men escaped, and seven were captured, including Brown, who had been wounded. He recovered in time to be tried by the state of Virginia. He was hanged in December, 1859.

Public opinion was sharply divided about Brown. Some thought him a hero and a martyr to the cause of liberty. Others called him a thief and a common murderer. Others thought he was mad, although he seemed rational enough at his own trial and refused to allow a plea of insanity in his defense. The one thing everyone agreed upon was that he had made the tension between the free North and the slaveholding South worse than ever.

Slightly more than a year after John Brown's raid on Harper's Ferry, Abraham Lincoln was elected President of the United States. Lincoln was the candidate of the Republican Party, which had promised not to let slavery spread any further into the West. The South hated the Republican Party and all it stood for, but the North had more votes and Lincoln won anyway.

The election of Lincoln made many of the leaders of the South decide that it was no longer safe for a slaveholding state to stay in the United States. Several of these Southern states left the Union; they "seceded."

FIGHTING FOR FREEDOM: PART I

Basically, the North would not allow them to go, and the result was the great, four-year, bloody Civil War.

Did slavery cause the Civil War? That is a complicated question. One thing is clear. The presence of slavery in one part of the country and the absence of it in another part was the most important factor in the coming of the War. The Northerners had not suddenly become abolitionist, but they had become more sensitive to the question of slavery and whether it was right or wrong. That sensitivity was mostly created by the antislavery men and women, white and black, free and runaway, who had the courage to speak out and tell their story.

When he heard the news of the firing on Fort Sumter, the first real shots of the Civil War, Frederick Douglass wrote, "At last our proud Republic is overtaken. Our National Sin has found us out. . . ."

The first part of the struggle to end slavery was over. The second part would be war itself, and the slaves would play a major part in their own liberation.

CHAPTER 10

Fighting for Freedom: Part II

THREE SLAVES MOVED their paddles soundlessly through the water. It was night on the eastern coast of Virginia, and the guns of the Civil War were quiet for the time being. The war had started on April 12, 1861, and as the slaves' boat slipped silently through the dark on the evening of May 23, eleven Southern slave states had declared their independence from the United States. The United States government would not let them go. The war between North and South that had just begun would drag on for four bloody years, and it would end slavery forever in North America. But these three men in the boat just hoped it would end slavery for them.

They floated out of the dark toward the startled Union soldier who was on guard at Fort Monroe. The Yankees had captured this fort on the coast even though Virginia was part of the Confederate States of America, as the South was called. The guard challenged them with his rifle at the ready, but the three men in the boat were just runaways. The guard took them in. The problem of what to do with them was passed on to the commanding officer, General Benjamin F. Butler.

FIGHTING FOR FREEDOM: PART II

Ben Butler was from Massachusetts, where many abolitionists lived, but he was not an abolitionist. What to do with these runaways was a dilemma for him. They were legally someone else's property. The laws of the United States were still supposed to be in effect, and that included the Fugitive Slave Law. Some people thought Butler should return the runaways to their master.

No, Ben Butler decided, he would not return them. These men were "property," and he had the right to confiscate property belonging to rebels. General Butler called the slaves "contraband of war," and he kept them to work at the Fort. The phrase, "contraband of war," caught people's imagination. Throughout the war runaway slaves were often referred to as "contrabands."

Not everyone in the federal government felt the way General Butler did, not even Abraham Lincoln. The Union, as the North was usually called, did not really know what to do about slaves or slavery. Officially, the Northerners were *not* fighting to end slavery. They were fighting to keep the United States together and to bring back the Southern states that were trying to leave.

Many people in the North did not care about slavery, even after all the years of runaway slaves and abolitionists. Besides, four slave states (Delaware, Maryland, Kentucky, and Missouri) were still in the Union. President Lincoln could not very well turn the war against the South into a war against slavery. It would have made too many people angry. At the beginning of the Civil War, the North was not yet ready to end slavery.

The runaways and free black people of the North wanted the war to be against slavery. They held meetings and passed resolutions and made speeches calling on the government to end slavery when they defeated the South. Frederick Douglass was one of the most outspoken people about this. Free black people throughout the United States pledged their help as soldiers to fight the South.

If the Union government under Lincoln did not even know what to do about three runaway slaves, however, they were surely not ready to recruit black people into the army, give them guns, and let them join the war against the South. Blacks who tried to join the army were turned away. In the beginning, the Union wanted to ignore the slaves and simply put the country back the way it was before Lincoln's election made the South secede.

The slaves of the South would not be ignored, however. The three men at Fort Monroe were just the first of hundreds, then thousands, then tens of thousands of slaves who ran away to reach the Northern army. For decades slaves had been running away to the North. Now the Northern army was coming to them. The word of the war quickly passed along the gossip grapevine of the slaves. They knew what was happening. It was the beginning of the end.

Alone or in huge groups, they came to the Union army camps. Some commanders sent the runaways back to their owners. Even Ben Butler did once, when he was in Louisiana. Others wanted to keep the slaves as workers. Some commanders put the runaways in refugee camps until they could figure out what to do with them. These camps were pretty horrible, crowded and dirty and unhealthy, with not enough food, but the runaways kept coming. One Union colonel said that every time his troops advanced, slaves would come swarming out from everywhere to get to his lines and be "free" from their master. "It is like putting your walking stick into an anthill," he said.

John Parker was one runaway. When the war began his master and master's two sons left the plantation near Richmond, Virginia, and an overseer took charge of the slaves. Then the overseer left to join the army, too. The slaves were sent to work on defense fortifications at several places. Then John Parker and his friends were ordered to help the Southern army in its first big battle against the Yankees at Bull Run.

Along with four other slaves, Parker was assigned to help an artillery battery. The guns began firing at ten in the morning, and all day Parker was loading the huge lead shot and swabbing out the barrel of the cannon after each round was fired. Yankee shells began to come down on them. A nearby battery was hit, and twenty men were killed. Many ran away in fear. John Parker stayed. "I was so excited that I hardly knew what I was about, and felt worse than dead," he remembered. He hoped the Union would win, but he was afraid for his own life in the battle. He wanted to run, but the white soldiers would shoot him down. He was trapped, helping to fight for the South and the slavery of his own people.

The South won the battle of Bull Run that day, but Parker's unit retreated. He helped bury the dead before he went. He was sent home.

When he got back to the plantation, the crops were in

Slaves fleeing to the Union lines during the Civil War, in North Carolina.

bad shape from neglect and the cattle had wandered off. Order was breaking down. This was his chance. He actually ran away twice, once to get to the Union lines and get a pass for his wife, and then a second time, after he had gone back to give the papers to her. They became separated. Finally Parker crossed the Potomac River way up near Frederick, Maryland, and was welcomed to freedom by the Union soldiers. The last we know of Parker he was on his way to New York to try to find his wife and their two girls. Two other children of his had to be left behind in the South.

Thomas Cole, a runaway from Alabama, found it was scary to be in battle even on the Yankee side. He had been running and hiding in the woods for days, living on fish and rabbits, when the Union soldiers found him. At first they treated him like a spy and asked him all kinds of questions, but he satisfied them that he was just a runaway. Like Parker, they had him helping with the cannons.

Cole was caught in one of the fiercest battles of a fierce war, at Chickamauga, Tennessee. He helped put the guns in place on a mountainside, and then, without warning, the firing started. Cole tried to hide in a hole in the ground. A Union soldier kicked him and ordered him to get up and help with the cannon. The battle grew hotter. "There was men laying, wanting help, wanting water, with blood running out them and the top or sides of their heads gone, great big holes in them." He wished he were back safe on the plantation, and prayed that if the Lord would help him he wouldn't run away any more.

Cole never returned home. He was finally sent to the rear of the lines to help with the wounded. He was scared and homeless, but now he had a way to earn his keep, and he was free.

Parker and Cole were just two of thousands of runaways, and the smart Union commanders made use of their help even if the blacks couldn't be soldiers yet. "Contrabands" cooked food and cleaned guns. They built forts and moved equipment. They repaired railroads and sewed uniforms. Some slaves were put to work on the plantations the Southerners had deserted, and the crops these refugees raised helped to feed the other runaways and the army, too. Some runaways became scouts or spies, because they knew the country so well.

Allan Pinkerton, the famous detective who worked for Lincoln and directed much of the spying against the South, often used runaway slaves. One morning, for example, Pinkerton took time out from duties in his office to have a newly arrived group of runaways brought to him. He spent the morning questioning them and got a lot of useful information. His attention was particularly caught by one young man named John Scobell.

"He had a manly and intelligent bearing," Pinkerton said of Scobell, "and his straightforward answers . . . impressed me." Scobell was originally from Mississippi, but he had come to Virginia with his master. From there he had run away, although technically he had been set free and was no longer a slave. He could read and write, which was unusual for a slave, and he was extremely intelligent.

Pinkerton leaned forward and asked Scobell if he would be willing to take the risks of spying. Everyone knew the risks; if they caught you, they killed you. Scobell agreed. Pinkerton provided him with false papers, and Scobell went on a spying trip through Virginia. He spent time as a peddler, a laborer, and a cook, and all the time he was watching, asking, and learning. He returned to Washington later with valuable information.

Slaves who never ran away helped the Union army sometimes. They gave directions. They reported on Confederate troop movements. Many Union prisoners escaped with the help of slaves. The old runaway network by which the slaves had helped each other escape was used to help captured Yankees.

FIGHTING FOR FREEDOM: PART II

One of those Yankees was Lieutenant Hannibal Johnson from Maine. Captured in Virginia in May of 1864,
Johnson escaped from a Confederate prison camp with
three other officers on the night of November 20. The
prison was in Columbia, South Carolina, and the nearest
Union troops were more than two hundred miles away in
Tennessee.

Three days after their escape, the soldiers were lost.
They had been nearly discovered at least once. All they
had to eat was some dry corn they had found in the
fields. They had to have shelter and help. It was a
gamble, but there was only one thing to do. They had to
find a slave who would help them.

Fearful but desperate, they approached a slave cabin
after dark. The cabin was home to an entire slave family
who belonged to a Confederate officer named Boozier.
The family quickly took in the Union soldiers and fed
them. The slaves took the officers to the woods at dawn
and hid them. The slaves told the soldiers to wait for a
guide to come after dark.

Johnson and his friends hid all day, and the promised
guide came after dark. His name was Frank. He took
them seven miles, until they were safely beyond the
nearest town and on a lonely road. Then he left them.
They walked twenty-two miles that night. After hiding all
day, they went to another slave cabin.

For weeks the soldiers lived like that. They were guided
by Bob, George, Peter, Arthur, Jim, Vance, and many
others. No one turned them away. The soldiers were
hidden in corn cribs, fodder barns, sheds, the woods,
anywhere safe. They were well fed and never felt in

danger. "They could not do enough for us," Hannibal Johnson remembered. "God bless the poor slaves."

On January 5, 1865, the four escapees reached Union lines. Without the help of the slaves they never would have made it alive.

Some slaves took even more direct action than helping Yankees escape. Robert Smalls lived in Charleston, South Carolina, in the very heart of the Confederate states. (The war had started in Charleston, when the South fired on Fort Sumter out in the harbor.) Smalls was a boat pilot. He worked on a steamboat called the *Planter,* which carried supplies to the Confederate troops along the South Carolina coast.

On the evening of May 12, 1862, the Confederate officers who were assigned to the *Planter* left for the day, and put Smalls in charge, as usual. He was supposed to tend the boiler fire and get everything ready for the mission the next morning. *Planter* was to deliver some cannon to a fort near Charleston on the 13th. But when morning came, the boat would not be there.

Smalls had been planning this for months. He knew that off on the eastern horizon there were Yankee warships. These warships were blockading Charleston. That is, they were trying to stop ships from coming in and out with supplies for the Confederacy. Smalls was going to go out to those Northern ships.

A little after eight o'clock in the evening, Robert Smalls' family came to visit him on the ship. This was not unusual, and the guards on the docks thought nothing of it. Robert's brother, John, and John's family came to visit, too. So did a slave who worked on another boat.

FIGHTING FOR FREEDOM: PART II

In the pitch dark, after midnight, Robert Smalls and his brother carefully built up the fire in the *Planter*'s boilers. The steam pressure in the engine began to rise. By three in the morning, the sentries were all asleep and the little coastal steamer was ready. Smalls backed *Planter* away from the dock.

To get to the Union fleet out on the ocean, Smalls and his family had to go right past three heavily armed forts: Fort Sumter, Fort Moultrie, and Castle Pinckney. These forts had huge guns, guns which kept the Union fleet safely away from shore. These same guns could sink the *Planter* in a second. Smalls knew it, and his family knew it. They all agreed to go down with the ship and drown rather than be captured.

Smalls knew the sentries at the forts would see them, so he didn't even try to sneak out. That certainly would have tipped them off. Instead, he sailed boldly out as though he were supposed to. He knew the signal codes to blow on the steam whistle, and when he gave these signals, the sentries figured that *Planter* was on a secret night mission. Slowly, deliberately, trying not to arouse suspicion, Smalls steered his boat expertly out of the harbor, past the terrifying guns and the stone walls of the forts, and into the open sea.

Once clear of the harbor, the families rejoiced. They took down the Confederate flag and put a white flag in its place. Smalls poured on the steam and headed for freedom. What he did not know was that there was one more danger ahead.

Out in the Union fleet, on board the U.S. Navy vessel *Onward,* the watch gave the alarm. "All hands to quarters!'' From the deck the crew could see a large black object coming at them through the mist that covered the sea just before dawn. Fear went around the *Onward*'s deck. The crew was sure it was a Confederate ram ship loaded with gunpowder coming to crash into the *Onward,* explode, and sink her.

The *Onward*'s crew tried frantically to turn their ship. One sailor cursed and cried that they must go down with colors flying! The number three gun was almost swung into position and the crew was preparing to blast the ram. Suddenly a voice from the lookout called, ''I think I see a white flag!''

The surprised crew of the *Onward* stopped, and stared. Here came *Planter,* not some destructive ram. On her decks were Robert Smalls and his family, singing and shouting and whistling and jumping up and down. They were free.

We know what became of Robert Smalls. He was welcomed by the Union Navy, who valued his knowledge of the coastal waters. The Smalls family was given prize money for delivering a captured Confederate ship. Robert Smalls himself continued to pilot *Planter* and other vessels for the Union in that area. After the war, Smalls became a leading black politician in South Carolina.

With men like Smalls showing their intelligence and courage, and with thousands of slaves running away to Union lines and wanting to fight to free their friends and family left behind, how long could the North ignore slavery? How long before the war-weary North realized that here were thousands of fresh soldiers for their battered army? When would the North stop pretending that the country could be put back together the way it was? Slavery may not have been the only cause of the Civil War, but it was the most important. Slowly public opinion in the North came around to understand that winning the war meant getting rid of slavery, too.

The decision to make the Civil War a war on slavery was slow to come, and many people in the North had a hard time agreeing with it. A lot of white people were still prejudiced against blacks, and resented fighting a war to set them free. But every day the war went on, more and more Northerners believed that slavery had to go, and that that was one of the things they were fighting for.

President Abraham Lincoln was one of the first to see that slavery had to end, but he kept silent for a long time. Personally, he hated slavery. "If slavery is not wrong," he said, "nothing is wrong." And he respected black people, even though he was himself born in the slave state of Kentucky. With Lincoln as president, black people were welcome as guests at the White House for the first time in American history. Frederick Douglass was invited to visit the president. When he did, he was greeted, he said, as one gentleman greets another. "I tell you," Douglass reported of his visit to meet Lincoln, "I felt *big* there."

Why then didn't President Lincoln become an abolitionist and use the war from the beginning to destroy slavery? The answer is that he did not believe that being the president gave him the right to do as he pleased. Ending slavery was something the people would have to decide to do. And at the beginning of the Civil War the people of the United States were not ready to do this.

CAPTIVE BODIES, FREE SPIRITS

When he felt the time was ripe, however, President Lincoln did try to lead the nation against slavery. In late 1862 he declared that as president he would free all the slaves who lived in the rebellious South as of January 1, 1863. Now this meant that any slave state that left the Confederacy and came back into the Union before January 1 could keep slavery. It also meant that the four slave states who never left the Union could keep slavery. Even so, Lincoln took a dramatic step. All the slaves in the rebel states were to be set free—"emancipated"—on the first day of the New Year. People called this act Lincoln's "Emancipation Proclamation."

All over the North, black people waited for the day to come. So many of them had been slaves once, or had friends who had been. They knew that nearly four million people like themselves were still slaves. There was a lot wrong with the Emancipation Proclamation, they realized, but it was a start. New Year's Day drew nearer.

On January 1, slaves and ex-slaves were free. Blacks across the Northern states felt that the great day of jubilation had come at last. The Reverend Henry Turner, of Washington, DC, was part of a crowd at the offices of the *Evening Star,* the first newspaper to appear that day. Several people tried to grab the first copy of the paper, but a young man got it and ran off shouting for joy. The happy crowd shredded the next available paper because so many wanted to get it. Henry Turner got the third copy, badly torn but with the precious Emancipation Proclamation intact. He raced down the street clutching his prize.

The Emancipation Proclamation. Many printers and publishers put out fancy editions of Lincoln's famous proclamation of 1862. This one was done in Philadelphia.

CAPTIVE BODIES, FREE SPIRITS

When the people waiting for him saw him come running, they began cheering and ran to meet him. Lifting him up on their shoulders, they carried him to a platform where he could read the words they had awaited for so long. Breathless, Turner gave the paper to a friend to read. As the words declaring the slaves in the rebel South forever free were read to the crowd, "every kind of demonstration was going on," Turner remembered. "Men squealed, women fainted, dogs barked, white and colored people shook hands, songs were sung, and by this time cannons began to fire at the navy yards."

Meanwhile, up in Boston, Frederick Douglass and a huge crowd waited at a hall called the Tremont Temple. Douglass was but one of the speakers scheduled for that day, but the speeches were just to kill time. What everyone was waiting for was word that Lincoln had gone through with the Proclamation as promised. A line of messengers was set up from the Temple to the telegraph office, ready to rush the news to the great meeting.

Nine o'clock in the evening came with no news from Washington. Ten o'clock came and went, and there was still silence. A depression fell over the crowd which all the eloquent speeches in the world could not help. It was a Judge Russell who had the honor of being the first with the news, and the reaction was the same as in Washington. The meeting broke up at midnight and immediately reassembled in the Twelfth Baptist Church, where it went on until dawn.

FIGHTING FOR FREEDOM: PART II

The Emancipation Proclamation was not the end of slavery. Technically it set free only those slaves in the Confederacy, and the Union government could not control the Confederacy. The Proclamation was a big step, however, and it gave people hope for what was still to come. The most important thing after the Proclamation was winning the war itself.

With the Civil War dragging on and on with no end in sight, people in the North began to change their minds about letting black soldiers join the army. After all, black men had been serving in the navy, so why not the army? Although a lot of people still objected, the army changed its mind late in 1862 and began to accept black recruits.

The black soldiers were kept by themselves, in all-black units. The officers were almost always white. Given the chance, black people joined the army by the thousands. By the end of the Civil War, over 186,000 black troops had served the Union. Nearly half of these men had been slaves. Many had gone directly from the plantation to the Northern army.

The white people of the Union wanted to know whether ex-slaves made good soldiers. "Loyal whites have generally become willing that they (the blacks) should fight," said one New York newspaper, "but the great majority have no faith that they will really do so." The first major battle involving black troops should have put all such worries to rest.

Port Hudson was a Confederate stronghold on the Mississippi north of New Orleans. The Union had captured New Orleans, but they could not move north to control the great river until they took Port Hudson. Under the command of General Nathaniel P. Banks, two regiments of free blacks and ex-slaves from Louisiana attacked Port Hudson on May 27, 1863. One of the regiments, called the Native Guard, was unusual because even the officers were black.

May 27 was hot, and the red dust of Louisiana rose in clouds as the soldiers began a nearly impossible charge across open ground toward the fort. The Confederate defenders opened up with musket and cannon. At every step, more of the attacking troops fell. The charge was stopped, but the day was not over. A second time, the black soldiers of Louisiana advanced into terrifying fire. A foot-thick tree toppled onto one company of soldiers, cut through the trunk by a cannon ball. Captain André Callioux, one of the black officers, was out in front of his men leading the charge with his left arm dangling uselessly, broken above the elbow by a musket ball. A cannon shell killed him.

Port Hudson was not taken that day. Six charges in all were turned back by the gunfire from the fort. Many, many men had fallen. But what the black soldiers had won that day was respect, respect from others and for themselves. No one who knew of Port Hudson could ever again doubt that slave soldiers could fight. One white officer said, "You have no idea how my prejudices with regard to negro troops have been dispelled by the battle the other day. The brigade of negroes behaved magnificently and fought splendidly; could not have done better."

A few weeks later, at Milliken's Bend, Mississippi, 600

black soldiers were attacked at three in the morning by 2,500 Confederate troops. The fighting was so fierce that it came down to hand-to-hand combat. The Confederate soldiers charged with bayonets on the end of their empty rifles.

A white officer with the black soldiers at Milliken's Bend wrote home. "I never more wish to hear the expression, 'the niggers won't fight.' Come with me 100 yards from where I sit, and I can show you the wounds that cover the bodies of 16 . . . brave, loyal and patriotic soldiers. . . . It was a horrible fight, the worst I was ever engaged in." Far more died than the sixteen soldiers who were that man's friends, but Milliken's Bend did not fall. The black troops held. The Assistant Secretary of War later wrote that their bravery completely changed the feeling that black troops could not be trusted.

Even before Milliken's Bend, black soldiers from the Fifty-Fourth Massachusetts attacked Fort Wagner, on Morris Island, South Carolina. Like Port Hudson, Fort Wagner was too well defended to be taken, but the Fifty-Fourth made a name for itself that day. One of the young men there was Frederick Douglass's son, Lewis. He wrote to his girlfriend, "Men fell all around me. A shell would explode and clear a space of twenty feet, our men would close up again, but it was no use. . . ."

Before the Civil War was over, black soldiers had fought in 449 battles, big and small. Over 37,000 died. Seventeen black soldiers and four black sailors were given the nation's highest military decoration, the Congressional Medal of Honor.

The risks for black soldiers were, in one way, higher

than for whites. The Southern soldiers would usually not treat defeated black soldiers as prisoners of war but as runaway slaves trying to rebel. Instead of taking them prisoner, the Confederates would shoot them, and also sometimes the white officers who led them. The most notorious such massacre was at Fort Pillow, Tennessee, on April 12, 1864. A Union force of 570 was overrun by Confederate troops. About half the union force was black. Even though the defenders of the fort surrendered, the Confederate troops shot many of them in cold blood after the battle.

What happened to the slaves who stayed home, who did not run away, or fight for the Union? Did they all hate slavery and their masters, and want to leave? Clearly, no. Many slaves had built a life of their own within the plantation system. Many cared for the white people with whom they lived and worked. They would not help the Union soldiers. The South was their home, and while they may not have liked slavery, they liked even less the huge armies in blue who swept across the land destroying everything in front of them. Many slaves protected their master's family while he was off at war, hiding valuables from the Yankees and trying to keep the farm or plantation going.

One of the things that worried the Southern leaders the most was how to keep control of the slaves while so many of the slaveowners were away at war. They believed the slaves as a group were not to be trusted. Too many times a master was surprised when a loyal slave turned out to be not so loyal, after all. A Richmond,

FIGHTING FOR FREEDOM: PART II

Virginia, man, for example, was startled one day when his slave coachman came downstairs dressed in the master's best clothes, with the master's cane and even his best watch. The slave announced that he had heard that Lincoln had set all the slaves free, and from now on, master could just drive his own coach!

Perhaps the attitude of many slaves is shown in the story of one young Tennessee runaway who joined the Union army. When he got a leave for a few days, he went to see his old mistress. She was glad to see him. She asked, "You remember when you were sick and I had to bring you to the house and nurse you?" "Yes'm," the soldier told her, "I remember." Angrily the white woman then said, "And now you are fighting me!" "No'm, I ain't fighting you," the soldier said, "I'm fighting to be free."

The Confederacy tried to fight a long, bloody war without using any of their millions of slaves and free blacks as soldiers. Near the end of the war, in desperation, they thought of doing this. General Robert E. Lee was in favor of it. He needed the extra troops badly. Lee advised that if any slaves would fight for the Confederacy, they should be given their freedom.

Certainly the Confederate troops had faced enough black soldiers on the other side to know that they could fight. So at the very end of the war, the Confederacy was making a last, feeble attempt to raise slave soldiers and train them to fight for the South. It was too late.

In time, with the help of tens of thousands of black soldiers, the Union forces wore down the fierce but overpowered Confederacy. More and more territory fell to the Union. Early in 1865, the Confederate capital at Richmond was captured. Some of the first troops to enter the city were black. Not too long after, General Robert E. Lee decided that no more men should have to die in a hopeless cause. In April, 1865, four years after it had begun, the Civil War was over.

Slavery was finished in America. After more than two centuries of human captivity, the United States did away with it. The adoption of the Thirteenth Amendment to the Constitution made it official. There would be plenty of trouble to come for both black and white Americans as they tried to work out new arrangements for living with each other, but after 1865 slavery was no longer in the way.

Even in the moment of triumph over slavery, there was tragedy. Only days after Lee surrendered, Abraham Lincoln was shot. John Wilkes Booth, who sympathized with the South, killed the president with a bullet to the head as Lincoln attended the theater. The whole nation was shaken by grief, even many Southerners, but no one felt the loss any more greatly than the blacks. Many of them had come to regard Lincoln as "Father Abraham," and saw in him a kind, patient, and powerful friend. Now he was dead.

Wednesday, April 19, 1865, was the date of the funeral at the White House. Forty thousand people lined the streets of Washington, DC, to watch the coffin pass on its way to the Capitol after the services. A detachment of black soldiers was to be part of the funeral procession. They had just rushed up from their duty station in Petersburg, Virginia, hoping to be in time to honor

Lincoln. When they arrived to find their place in the line of march, it was already two o'clock, time for the parade to start. The streets were packed. There was no way to get to the back of the line without reorganizing everything. There was only one thing to do—let them march at the front.

So it was that in the final year of slavery in America, at the funeral of the fallen leader who had helped end slavery and held the country together, the place of honor was held by the Twenty-second U.S. Colored Infantry. For the slaves who had helped to build this country, for Henry Brown and Ibrahima and Frederick Douglass and Harriet Tubman and millions of others, it was a fitting moment.

Suggested Further Readings

Alford, Terry. *A Prince Among Slaves.* Tells the story of one slave, from his childhood in Africa to his fortuitous return to his homeland in old age.

Aptheker, Herbert. *American Negro Slave Revolts.* Millwood, NY: Kraus Reprint, 1978. This was originally published in 1943, but is still useful.

Blassingame, John. *The Slave Community: Plantation Life in the Ante-Bellum South.* New York: Oxford University Press, 1979. Covers slavery from the perspective of the slave.

Douglass, Frederick. *The Life and Times of Frederick Douglass.* Secaucus, NJ: Citadel Press, 1984. A classic.

Duff, John B. and Peter M. Mitchell, eds. *The Nat Turner Rebellion: The Historical Event and the Modern Controversy.* Handy.

Franklin, John Hope. *From Slavery to Freedom: A History of Negro Americans.* New York: Alfred Knopf, 1980. The standard text by the dean of Afro-American historians.

Frazier, E. Franklin. *The Negro Family in the United States.* Chicago: University of Chicago Press, 1966. A standard text.

SUGGESTED FURTHER READINGS

Mannix, Daniel R. *Black Cargoes: A History of the Atlantic Slave Trade, 1518-1865.* A good general account of slavery.

McPherson, James. *The Negro's Civil War: How American Negroes Felt & Acted during the War for the Union.* Champaign, IL: University of Illinois Press, 1982. A fascinating account told mostly in the participants' own words.

Quarles, Benjamin. *Black Abolitionists.* A fine treatment.

——. *The Negro in the American Revolution.* New York: W. W. Norton, 1973. Covers the subject extremely well. The same author's *The Negro in the Civil War* is equally outstanding.

Rose, Willie Lee. *A Documentary History of Slavery in North America.* New York: Oxford University Press, 1976. An excellent compendium of original sources.

Stampp, Kenneth M. *The Peculiar Institution: Slavery in the Ante-Bellum South.* New York: Alfred Knopf, 1956. The best single serious work on slavery.

Wade, Richard C. *Slavery in the Cities: The South, 1820-1860.* New York: Oxford University Press, 1965. Covers well that often overlooked aspect of the subject.

In the 1930s, Works Progress Administration (WPA) interviewers took down the reminiscences of ex-slaves. These narratives are used in many works. *Great Slave Narratives* by Arna Bontemps and *Lay My Burden Down,* edited by B. A. Botkin, are two such books.

Index

INDEX

INDEX